Traumatic Possessions

Traumatic Possessions

The Body and Memory in African American
Women's Writing and Performance

JENNIFER L. GRIFFITHS

University of Virginia Press

CHARLOTTESVILLE AND LONDON

University of Virginia Press

Printed in the United States of America on acid-free paper

First published 2009

9 8 7 6 5 4 3 2 1

LIBRARY OF CONGRESS CATALOGING-IN-PUBLICATION DATA

Griffiths, Jennifer L., 1968–

  Traumatic possessions : the body and memory in African American women's writing
and performance / Jennifer L. Griffiths.

      p.   cm.

  Includes bibliographical references and index.

  ISBN 978-0-8139-2883-8 (cloth : alk. paper)

  ISBN 978-0-8139-2884-5 (pbk. : alk. paper)

  ISBN 978-0-8139-2895-1 (e-book)

    1. American literature—African American authors—History and criticism.

2. American literature—Women authors—History and criticism.   3. Psychic trauma

in literature.   4. Human body in literature.   5. Memory in literature.   6. African

American women in literature.   I. Title.

PS153.N5G75   2010

810.9'9287'08996—dc22

                                                                    2009023626

A book in the American Literatures Initiative (ALI), a collaborative
publishing project of NYU Press, Fordham University Press, Rutgers
University Press, Temple University Press, and the University of Virginia
Press. The Initiative is supported by The Andrew W. Mellon Foundation.
For more information, please visit www.americanliteratures.org.

Contents

Preface

While working on this manuscript, I attended a conference titled "Psychological Trauma: Attachment, Neuroscience, and Body Experience," hosted by Bessel van der Kolk's Boston-based Trauma Center. As I sat in the crowded auditorium, I engaged in conversation with the participants around me, most of whom spent their working days as social workers, art therapists, and psychologists. The conversation turned to my interest, as a humanities scholar, in traumatized individuals. Instead of trying to describe the issues of representation, the struggle for language, and the inescapability of traumatic repetition, I found myself wanting to redirect the conversation to hear more from them about the pursuit of recovery. For them, when interacting with trauma survivors, recovery is always the goal. And recovery's starting point involves making meaning from the body's complex and often contradictory messages. At one notable moment, I remember hearing Bessel van der Kolk making an offhand remark when addressing the crowd; he referred to the theater group with which he had worked, making the claim that they had discovered what was in his view the most promising strategy for dealing with the body's role in recovery from trauma. No longer was language the key to recovery; "talk therapy," it seems, addresses only part of the equation and does not account for implicit memory, the body-based resonance of traumatic experience.

The playwrights and writers examined in *Traumatic Possessions* challenge the division of body and voice, or implicit and declarative memory, by looking at the survival experience across temporal and spatial boundaries. Their search for a more complete understanding of the past leads them to the body, the site of both cultural inscription and traumatic experience, to develop creative strategies to confront the neglect, distortion, and regulation of traumatic memory, specifically in relation to the split that occurs between image, body, and voice.

These creative productions share the discovery made by the clinicians that the body matters when recovering from traumatic experience. However, the writers complicate this understanding by looking at the body as inscribed within a racialized cultural script. In each text, there are moments when the survivor attempts to make a public statement and to put into language the struggle that traumatic experience has imposed on her soul. Dessa in her jail cell, Rodney King in the video frame, Sally on the auction block, Venus in the courtroom, and Ursa in her own family history—each character must negotiate the limits placed on their bodies in an effort to speak their truths. They must first acknowledge and accommodate within their testimony what Fanon refers to as "the fact of blackness," specifically as it informs their ability to create testimony in a public sphere that marks their difference.

Moving away from language-based memory and testimony alone may not be the end but the beginning of movement out of the isolation that is the essence of traumatic experience. And finding true witnesses requires an acknowledgment of the problems found within intersubjective dynamics when racism precludes connection. The cultural projects examined in *Traumatic Possessions* offer a new direction for trauma studies as a field of academic inquiry. By returning the body as a site of possibility, Jones, Smith, Williams, Parks, and McCauley each and all reconfigure the trajectory of trauma studies, with its emphasis on the limits of language and the inescapability of repetition, to a more hopeful place.

Acknowledgments

I started thinking more concretely about this acknowledgments section as the 2:34 p.m. train left Grand Central one Tuesday afternoon in late January '09. The early research for this study occurred during another period of Metro North commuting when I attended the CUNY Graduate Center as a doctoral candidate in English. I begin, then, by thanking my friends and mentors at the Grad Center, most especially Meena Alexander, who served as midwife (her words) to my early development as a scholar and who continues to serve as my model for leading a life devoted to the pursuit of intellectual, creative, and social-justice-related truths. My dear friend Wendy Ryden has provided more intellectual and emotional sustenance than I can account for here, and I am grateful for her supportive friendship during this process. Kathy Cooke and Dave Valone have kept me focused in moments of doubt and energized when I thought it all impossible. I wish also to thank Jill Dolan, Norman Kelvin, Sondra Perl, and Neal Tolchin for their guidance and constructive feedback along the way.

My experience with the University of Virginia Press was fruitful and seamless thanks to the professionalism of Cathie Brettschneider, and I wish to express my appreciation for her efforts here as well.

Although the train remains the same, the commute now involves a different destination. When I arrive at New York Institute of Technology's Manhattan campus at 1855 Broadway, I am greeted daily by an amazingly diverse and exciting group of students and colleagues. I would like to express my gratitude to my students and colleagues in the NYIT

English Department, especially to Kathy Williams and Michael Schiavi, who have provided considerable support as I faced the challenges of balancing tenure-track responsibilities with my dedication to this project.

The life at the other end of the Metro North line provides the primary motivation for all good things I do in this life. My family—particularly my mother, Carole Scillia; my sister, Carolyne Cebrian; my great-aunt Margaret Doolan; my father, Tom Griffiths; and the Suntags—has made it possible for me to immerse myself in an extensive study of traumatic legacies without feeling isolated or overwhelmed. I am most deeply grateful to the two individuals who have given me the greatest sense of connection to life's larger purpose, my son, Rody James Conway, and my daughter, Helaine Margaret Griffiths. They have been so patient at the New Haven end of the train line, and this book is dedicated to them.

An earlier version of chapter 3 was published in *Frontiers: A Journal of Women's Studies*. Chapter 4 is a revision of an essay that first appeared in *Studies in the Novel*. I thank both journals for their cooperation in allowing me to include revised versions of these pieces in *Traumatic Possessions*.

Introduction

In *Testimony: Crises of Witnessing in Literature, Psychoanalysis, and History*, Dori Laub describes a videotaped archive of a Holocaust survivor recounting a Jewish rebellion at Auschwitz. "She was," Laub writes, "relating her memories as an eyewitness of the Auschwitz uprising; a sudden intensity, passion and color were infused into the narrative. She was fully there."[1] In the tape, which Laub presents to an interdisciplinary conference, the woman remembers four chimneys exploding. After the conference screening, the historians in the audience protest the accuracy of her testimony because, in fact, only one chimney had been destroyed. For Laub, this factual discrepancy does not discredit the testimony. The historians in their judgment fail to recognize the emotional and psychological dimensions of testimony. The event had happened in several ways simultaneously. The survivor's perspective offers insight into the magnitude of the event in the lives and memories of the individuals most intimately affected by it.

The Laub anecdote raises crucial questions about the body, witnessing, and the creation of testimony. Since trauma evades conscious understanding, memory becomes encoded on a bodily level and resurfaces as possession. According to trauma experts such as Judith Herman and Bessel van der Kolk, the survivor relives the original experience through a body memory yet struggles to find words for an experience that exceeds representation. A kind of break between body and language occurs that, as Laub suggests, only a connection to another body can bridge. Laub explains, "Massive trauma precludes its registration; the observing and recording mechanisms of the human mind are temporarily knocked out, malfunction. . . . While historical evidence to the event which constitutes the trauma may be abundant and documents in vast supply, the trauma—as a known event and not simply as overwhelming shock—has not been truly witnessed yet, not been taken cognizance of."[2]

The event becomes known through the process of telling the story to a listener, "who is . . . the blank screen on which the event comes to be inscribed for the first time." Testimony, therefore, depends on a relationship and a process between the survivor and the witness, as memory emerges and reunites a body and a voice severed in trauma. These fractured pieces of the survivor's self come together in the reflection of the listener, and memory comes into meaning through this bodily transaction, rather than simply by creating a narrative in language. Laub asserts that "the absence of an empathic listener, or more radically, the absence of an addressable other, an other who can hear the anguish of one's memories and thus affirm and recognize their realness, annihilates the story."[3] The listener becomes an integral part of this awareness and the process of creating meaning from the chaos of trauma.

Testimony, therefore, exposes the vulnerability of listeners as well. They must face their limitations, their mortality, through the story of another's trauma. According to Laub, "The listener . . . has to be at the same time a witness to the trauma and a witness to himself. It is only in this way, through his simultaneous awareness of the continuous flow of those inner hazards both in the trauma witness and in himself, that he can become the enabler of testimony—the one who triggers its initiation, as well as the guardian of its process and of its momentum."[4] The testimonial encounter happens when the listener comprehends the bodily response accompanying the struggle for a language to express the chaos of trauma, such as in Laub's example when he reads the body of the Holocaust survivor while she tells her story.

Holocaust stories and the theory developed from them have achieved what Kay Schaffer and Sidonie Smith refer to as "paradigmatic status," providing "limit cases of trauma"; however, recent scholarship has challenged the notion of the Holocaust as a discrete event beyond comparison with other experiences of extreme human suffering.[5] Ana Douglass and Thomas A. Vogler claim in their introduction to *Witness and Memory: The Discourse of Trauma*, "The view that the Holocaust is unique and without parallel in human history is closer to a doctrine or a dogma than to a reasoned discursive position."[6] *Traumatic Possessions* is interested in this challenge to the Holocaust's "uniqueness" only in that it allows the theories about human response to traumatic experience developed by Holocaust scholars to illuminate other encounters with race-related trauma and its legacies. Although the earlier Laub anecdote comes from a Holocaust-related source, the issues it raises can offer a great deal when considering the act of testimony. This book works with contemporary developments in trauma studies, including the Holocaust-centered writings of Laub, Dominick LaCapra, and Cathy Caruth, as well as scholars, such as Judith Herman, who make connections to other sites of extreme suffering and who explore the relational nature of recovery.

Beginning with the scene of Laub's Auschwitz survivor, *Traumatic Possessions* asks, what happens when we insert another body into the conference scene and include questions about race into the discussion around intersubjectivity and the witnessing encounter so central to trauma studies, which begins with Holocaust trauma narratives such as the Laub anecdote as the dominant paradigm. Indeed, *Traumatic Possessions* focuses on the intersubjective dynamic involved in the creation of testimony after trauma, specifically dealing with the alterations and complications of this relationship as it relates to the black female post-traumatic experience across generations and cultural contexts.

When attempting to examine the representation of African American experience using contemporary trauma theories, scholars must address—and recently have addressed—certain concerns about the usefulness of these critical tools. Although trauma theories have their roots in Freudian psychoanalysis and "the Western trope of trauma" involving Holocaust studies,[7] current postcolonial and critical race scholarship[8] has challenged the position that these theories offer no possibilities for understanding more universal aspects of human suffering. Writing on W. E. B. Du Bois and trauma, Christina Zwarg addresses specifically the reluctance to apply psychoanalytic readings to African American texts but then claims, "the emergence of 'trauma studies' has made it possible to reenlist psychoanalysis in the work of cultural critique."[9] For Zwarg and other critics, trauma studies works in the gaps revealed by Freud's abandonment of seduction theory[10] and allows a critique of classical psychoanalysis's patriarchal, Eurocentric biases. According to Zwarg, "The haunting power of trauma has to do with the ambivalence Freud feels toward the concept from the moment he separates himself from the seduction theory by cutting trauma roughly in half, brilliantly elaborating the symbolic resonances and somewhat hastily (though never completely) obscuring the psychic burden of actual events."[11] Identifying this detour away from the historical event as one of "the shortcomings of the classical psychoanalytic model of trauma," J. Brooks Bouson supports Zwarg's assessment and recent scholarship that "find[s] the source of the dissociated memories that haunt the trauma survivor not in repressed feelings and fantasies but in actual events."[12] Like Zwarg, Brooks Bouson sees Freud's blind spot as the point at which he disowns his previous assertions about the pervasiveness of sexual abuse in the lives of his female patients, or the moment he refuses to bear witness to their trauma as such. This gap provides for recent trauma theorists an opportunity to dismantle the classical psychoanalytic model's emphasis on repression and desire and to focus more directly on the impact of the actual traumatic event on the historical subject. In this way, these theories, when applied to African American traumatic experience, do not threaten to elide the suffering caused by the actual events and material conditions of institutionalized racism.

If contemporary trauma theory marks a departure from Freud by including a possible deconstruction of the classical psychoanalytic model, trauma studies can answer Hortense Spillers's call for a "psychoanalytic cultural criticism, or psychoanalytics" that "would establish the name of inquiry itself as the goal of an interior intersubjectivity . . . as the locus at which self-interrogation takes place. It would not be an arrival but a departure, not a goal but a process, and it conduces toward neither an answer nor a cure because it is not engendered in formulae and prescriptions."[13] For Spillers, "'Race' speaks through multiple discourses that inhabit intersecting axes of relations that banish once and for all the illusion of a split between 'public' and 'private.'"[14] Heeding Spillers's call could entail examining the meeting between the "intersecting axes of relations" of race and the intersubjectivity of the witnessing encounter.

Although this study considers the way recent theories on traumatic experience describe the survivor's direct internal experience, particularly around the complications of memory, its primary focus entails the transmission of this experience and the problems that arise when this transmission occurs within a racialized public space. Drawing on the work of Piotr Sztompka and "allowing for the centrality of mediation and imaginative reconstruction," Ron Eyerman asserts, "one should perhaps not speak of traumatic events, but rather of traumatic affects. While trauma refers necessarily to something experienced in psychoanalytic accounts, calling this experience 'traumatic' requires interpretation."[15] This "interpretation" does not happen between two ideologically pure individuals; rather, it occurs within what Laurence Kirmayer refers to as "landscapes of memory," or "the metaphoric terrain that shapes the distance and effort required to remember affectively charged and socially defined events that initially may be vague, impressionistic, or simply absent from memory."[16] The shifting terrains or landscapes of memory provide the ground on which the witnessing encounter, as described by Laub, occurs. This work focuses on the survivor's body within these shifting and varied landscapes and specifically on the interactions between the black female body as a site of inscription for cultural values and the body as source of the memories in the production of testimony.

Testimony offers a public enactment of memory, and clearly, the cultural context and content work collaboratively to shape testimony. When looking at the reception of testimony within specific contexts, one must also consider cultural inscriptions of identity onto the body. How we mark different bodies is linked to the transmission and reception of memory and testimony. Survivors, in attempting to place their experience into words, must confront language itself and their position within dominant sign system. Discussions of the testimonial encounter, however, seldom reflect on the ideological pull of image and text, the inscription of identity through language, and the marking of bodies within a racial and gender schema. In the case of Laub's story one might ask, how does gender affect the audience's perception of the survivor? Would her agitation have been read differently if she did not express it through a female body? Would the audience have paused a moment more before discrediting her? What happens when testimony occurs in a public space through the body of a woman? Or the racialized body? How does the spectacle of these "othered" bodies interfere with the transmission of testimony?

In *Traumatic Possessions* the "landscapes of memory" or the cultural contexts in which testimony emerges and is processed by survivor and witness all involve race relations within the United States, specifically around the traumatic legacies of the black female body in U.S. history. Judith Herman makes connections between different populations when discussing trauma, and this book gains inspiration from her earlier work, which makes important connections between cultural, historical, and personal realms. Laub's survivor story asks us to look at the importance of testimony but also shows the way testimonial encounters are transactions between individuals and make public the private knowledge of trauma. This understanding of trauma is particularly interesting when it is considered in relation to other histories, or other points and places when the subject position of both survivor and listener-witness conflict, influencing the translation of the event into meaningful knowledge.

T. Denean Sharpley-Whiting invokes Frantz Fanon's well-known description of the black body as "overdetermined from without" in her study of the Venus Hottentot spectacle and legacy. For Sharpley-Whiting, this speculative process marks the black female body as "a phobic object," causing black female subjects to become "perpetually ensnared, imprisoned in an essence of themselves created from without."[17] How do these discursive limits, including this phobia, control the process by which this body comes into meaning around the testimony of trauma? How can a person whose body evokes dread and irrational fear within the dominant public imagination gain a just hearing when trying to piece together the fragmented post-traumatic experience?

To return to an oft-quoted scene from *Black Skin, White Masks*, Frantz Fanon describes the painful dichotomy between his body as he experiences it and as it functions within white colonialist perception, which he refers to as the "historico-racial schema." In the scene, when a young white child points to Fanon and yells, "Look, a Negro!" he sets in motion a dynamic that reproduces racist ideologies denying black subjectivity. Fanon writes,

> My body was given back to me sprawled out, distorted, recolored, clad in mourning in that white winter day. The Negro is an animal, the Negro is bad, the Negro is mean, the Negro is ugly; look, a nigger, it's cold, the nigger is shivering, the nigger is shivering because he is cold, the little boy is trembling because he is afraid of the nigger, the nigger is shivering with cold that goes through your bones, the handsome little boy is trembling because he thinks the nigger is quivering with rage, the little white boy throws himself into his mother's arms: Mamma, the nigger's going to eat me up.[18]

Racism succeeds on the basis of its ability to distort the experience of individuals dehumanized and traumatized under its logic, as Fanon's scene attests. Fanon's body, his "corporal schema," is replaced in this scene by the "historico-racial schema," or the mark of colonial history inscribed on his body and reproduced through these interactions with white perception. Fanon reveals a reflexive and violent reading of the black body that silences and distorts his experience. How then would this reading preclude the possibility of testimony, in which the survivor's body requires a listener, a "blank screen" on which to inscribe its struggling speech? How can the subjectivity of the "othered" survivor emerge in a public space that aligns him or her with corporeality and denies what Bibi Bakare-Yusuf refers to as "the possession of a voice" in public space.[19] In a public sphere that always seeks to maintain the hegemony of masculinity and whiteness, what happens to the reconstitution of the traumatized subject through testimony, which must always be publicly enacted to transform the isolation of traumatic experience?

As Houston Baker suggests in his essay "Scene . . . Not Heard," the public reception of testimony from people of color has created a rigid dichotomy between body and voice. Historically, people of color have entered the public space in body only. Marked already sexually and racially other within dominant cultural ideology, their displayed bodies presented their stories. Baker describes use of the voiceless body in testimonies of racial violence: "For the slave—even when he or she is a 'fugitive' from southern violence—is expected to remain silent. At northern abolitionist rallies, for example, the fugitive becomes the 'Negro exhibit.' She silently turns her back to the audience in order to display the stripes inflicted by the southern overseer's whip."[20] The public reads the stories told through "silent display." The image of a damaged black female body enters the public consciousness without a voice, a silent object in the performance, and her body-as-text conforms to fit seamlessly within a cultural script that already marks her as "Other."

In her introduction to *Twilight: Los Angeles, 1992*, theater artist Anna Deavere Smith provides a scene from a crisis in contemporary life in which a survivor's body and voice remain severed from each other and the ability to perceive the suffering of another human being is hindered dramatically by racial difference:

> For jurors in Simi Valley, Rodney King appeared to be a threat to the police. Moreover, he had been speeding. The officers were, as far as they were concerned, enforcing the law. Police officers reportedly concluded that King was on the drug PCP, impervious to pain, and therefore not responding to the beating. On the other hand, when I interviewed Rodney King's aunt, she burst into tears as she recounted seeing the beating on television, and "hearing him holler." She heard King's cries the first time she saw the tape. Yet a juror in the federal civil rights trial against the officers who also heard King's reactions to the police blows told me that the rest of the jury had difficulty hearing what she and King's aunt had heard. But when, during the deliberations, they focused on the audio rather than the video image, their perspective changed. The physical

image of Rodney King had to be taken away for them to agree that he was in pain and responding to the beating.[21]

Whereas Laub's historians could not see beyond their epistemological boundaries, in this case there is a jury that could not see King simultaneously as a human being capable of suffering under the heavy, relentless blows and as a large black man. The meaning of the scene had been determined before the jurors had entered the courtroom. Ironically, seeing and believing still carry evidentiary weight, but this time the believing seems to have preceded the seeing. The jurors equated, on some level, black masculinity solely with aggression that society must control, manage, tame. Only when they removed his body from the scene could they interpret it in any other way; only then could they connect the cries with human pain. In this case, visual artifact, and not King himself, tells the story of his beating. Yet even with this record of his suffering, proof that seems to have been required for the historians of Laub's anecdote, the survivor's story is interpreted within an ideological frame.

Elaine Scarry, who has noted the disparity between textual efforts to represent psychological suffering and physical pain, concludes that "no language for [physical] pain" exists and that the transmission of the experience to a witness includes its own "unmaking" of signification: "To have pain is to have *certainty*; to hear about pain is to have *doubt*."[22] Traumatic experience complicates the possibility of witness even further by involving a past wound that continues, on a bodily level, to distress the survivor in the present. Current trauma theories by Laub and Judith Herman acknowledge the leap to connection and toward overcoming doubt within the witnessing encounter, similar to what Dominick LaCapra refers to as empathic unsettlement.[23] However, as Scarry points out, the claim that "there is no language for pain" comes with real political implications: "The difficulty of articulating physical pain permits political and perceptual complications of the most serious kind. The failure to express pain—whether the failure to objectify its attributes or instead the failure, once those attributes are objectified, to refer them to their original site in the human body—will always work to allow its appropriation and conflation within debased forms of power."[24] Pointing out that in Scarry's seminal work on cultural pain studies "the relationship of pain to race and racism is never considered,"[25] Deborah Walker King inserts the black body into the discussion, examining the political implications that accompany the inexpressibility of pain when it occurs within the black body. King writes,

Contemporary black people, existing on the margins of society, become conflated in images of blackpain with the stereotypical black body, which is assumed to be pained, terrible, and unsafe. Blackpain, then, is a symbolic and intrusive abstraction of black people as living beings. As such, it is essential to the mythic logic of a pain-free American identity. Like their slave ancestors, African *Americans* and their assumed pained existence are threats to this logic. Black people cannot be both Americans and be pained.[26]

If, as King suggests, "images of suffering, dismembered, or disfigured black bodies function within a negative symbolic index of social worth defining what an American is *not*,"[27] how do we read the jury's inability to register suffering within the Rodney King case? To see his pain in the video allows this projection of suffering onto the other's body, but would hearing the cries release the jurors, who stand in for the dominant white society, from the "spell" of this projection?[28]

Although, arguably, jurors and historians have very specific and limited goals in their search for meaning, they represent cultural forces participating in the creation of a dominant narrative that has the potential either to reflect or to displace individual memory. In the case of the King video, the jurors created a narrative based on the scene of racial violence in which the black body always performs as perpetrator. King's voice is never heard, which, according to Baker, follows a continuum of silenced testimony from people of color in the public sphere. King's body, captured on video, speaks for him. His memory alone has no credibility in the court of law. Part of my project includes analyzing scenes of public testimony that regulate bodies and voices and the impact of this regulation on the process of witnessing. These scenes of public testimony locate trauma within a static body or voice. An incomplete memory, an "official story," filtered through a racist and sexist discourse, is offered to future generations. The official story does not account for the crisis of survival. This history making privileges a dominant declarative memory, the facts and figures of those members in the position to record them, and violently erases the experience of implicit memory, the collective bodily memory of trauma, which gets "bur[ied] . . . in the frightened fastness of the individual soul."[29] The dominant cultural voice performs a kind of dubbing over the scene of violence, imposing itself as the interpretative force and reinscribing oppression through the dislocation of body and voice.

What are the consequences of this rejection for the survivor, her ability to piece together experience in memory to reintegrate the self that has been fragmented by trauma? How can we see beyond the scene, revealing its construction within a racist framework? Judith Butler asks, "If racism pervades white perception, structuring what can and cannot appear within the horizon of white perception, then to what extent does it interpret in advance 'visual evidence'? And how, then, does such 'evidence' have to be read, and read publicly, against the racist disposition of the visible which will prepare and achieve its own inverted perceptions under the rubric of 'what is seen'?"[30] Bearing witness to the suffering of another involves exposing oneself and one's potential as victim, perpetrator, or accomplice. A kind of false witness occurs whenever the listener thwarts the creation of testimony to avoid its painful truths. This failure to provide an "addressable other" within collective space or cultural institutions reinscribes the mark of trauma onto the racialized or gendered body, thus containing trauma within this inscription and denying the vulnerability of the dominant symbolic order. This book focuses on the creative efforts to read testimony against dominant perception and to counter a landscape of memory that supports white supremacy or misogyny through selective memory, collective forgetting, and denial of testimony that would threaten its hegemony. Trauma fractures the symbolic order, and testimony restores a sense of connection for the survivor. In the performance and literary texts that I examine, the reconstitution of the self through testimony provides an opportunity to challenge the dominant symbolic order and to challenge the "historico-racial schema" or the cultural inscription that silences the voices of survivors.

In this pursuit, I join other scholars, writers, and artists who examine the lingering consequences of the "historico-racial schema" for the black female subject within cultural scripts corrupted by white-supremacist ideologies. Representative of this work, texts such as *Recovering the Black Female Body: Self-Representations by African American Women* focus on the writers Nella Larsen, Pauline Hopkins, and Lucille Clifton and their efforts to represent black female critical awareness and reclaiming of a bodily self. Many of the essays in that collection explore the legacy of unacknowledged, systemic violence and degradation of the black female body in law, popular culture, photojournalism, and literature. To these scholars, criticism functions as a restorative gesture. For example, Yvette Louis explores the way Suzan-Lori Parks's work challenges "dominant discourses that have pathologized the black body and represents a counternarrative of the black body as the source of abundance."[31]

Emphasizing the "black female body as a discursive body," Louis suggests, "Perhaps the best place to begin a reinvention of the construction of black womanhood, through representations of the black female body, is in recuperating and reinterpreting the history of slavery."[32] *Traumatic Possessions* does indeed follow this recommendation and begins with the reenvisioning of the female slave body in Sherley Anne Williams's *Dessa Rose*.

Writers such as Sherley Anne Williams and Suzan-Lori Parks linger in the struggle for the subject to redefine herself within a symbolic order that accommodates traumatic experience even as that experience always forces the recognition of the limits of representation. A struggle—to listen to the body's voice, to process its information, and to move beyond the muting isolation of trauma—emerges in the texts examined in this study. Part of the task of moving away from the false projection of cultural anxiety onto survivors entails acknowledging the actual bodily experience of trauma, or telling the body's story, instead of inscribing a story onto the body.

Traumatic Possessions includes five chapters that focus on questions about testimony and traumatic memory, both in body and in language. The playwrights and writers I have chosen challenge the division of body and voice, or implicit and declarative memory, by looking at the survival experience across temporal and spatial boundaries. De Certeau's suggestion that "memory is a sort of anti-museum: it is not localizable"[33] is borne out in the work of these writers. The challenge of articulating post-traumatic experience, particularly as it moves across generational and geographical borders, suggests an effort to address what Nicholas Abraham refers to as the "phantom," the residue of ancestral experience lingering in our presence, the truth that has acquired the weight of several lifetimes yet remains ungraspable. "Reducing the 'phantom,'" Abraham offers, "entails reducing the sin attached to someone else's secret and stating it in acceptable terms so as to defy, circumvent, or domesticate the phantom's (and our) resistances."[34] Performers Anna Deavere Smith and Robbie McCauley explore the limitations and possibilities of witnessing in a multiethnic public space, particularly in relation to the "secrets" and "sins" of historical racism. The performance texts explore the legacy of racism's "phantom" on present subjects, using the body to critique the spectacle of the gendered and racialized subject and to probe the discursive boundaries of embodiment and identity. In the literary texts I have chosen, Suzan-Lori Parks, Anna Deavere Smith, Robbie McCauley, Gayl Jones, and Sherley Anne Williams create experimental narrative strategies to explore the challenges in representing the complex connections between the memory, language, and the body in the testimony. Challenging traditional narratives that restrict form and content, they build new forms from memory fragments and bodily states. Like Ursa's improvisational blues or Dessa's jailhouse dreams, these forms include fantasy, temporal and spatial shifts, repetitions, and radical revision of the body's place in narrative.

The first two chapters include key historical and archetypal figures: a female slave and the Venus Hottentot. These figures experience direct trauma within the texts and must present their testimony to "experts" who reconstruct the traumatic event and its aftermath within the dominant discourse, using the trauma to reinforce the discursive limits placed on the black female body within a racialized public sphere. Chapter 1 introduces issues of cross-racial witnessing and the relationship between history and individual memory in Sherley Anne Williams's *Dessa Rose*. In the spaces of the plantation, auction block, and jail, memories emerge and become texts for reading and misreading the body's response to the unspeakable horrors of slavery. The chapter focuses specifically on the ways in which these memories counter and resist the "official" interpretations of Dessa's experience made in the court and by the white writer, Nehemiah, who repeatedly attempts to control Dessa's story and deny her subjectivity within the pages of the historical record he strives to create. In chapter 2, Suzan Lori Parks's play *Venus* provides insight into the traumatized body as public spectacle and invokes questions about agency, the erotic element of perpetrator-victim dynamics, and the production of cultural memory. This chapter also examines issues of agency by comparing critical responses to Parks's play with contemporary human-rights discourse on human trafficking.

The next two chapters address texts that deal with the legacies of these bodies, the inheritance by female bodies in the present as well as the individuals who witness the survivors' heirs struggle with this legacy. Chapter 3 uses Robbie McCauley's *Sally's Rape* to look at rape as a traumatic event that both separates and divides women across racial boundaries. "Pain is full of information," according to Robbie McCauley, who uses her own naked body to evoke a traumatic history and to reverse the internalization of shame and guilt by addressing the unspeakable and creating a space for possible dialogue. Chapter 4 focuses more thoroughly on issues related to the female body and cultural response to historical crisis, specifically in transgenerational trauma, in Gayl Jones's *Corregidora*. Informed by recent theories about the transgenerational transmission of traumatic experience, the chapter addresses the question of how trauma, in bodily memory and narrative, reproduces its own conditions and allows the female body to remain trapped in painful silence within individuals, family systems, and the community. How do writers such as Gayl Jones represent the unbearable weight of the testimony across generations and create an "addressable other" to counter the reproduction of traumatic experience and to transform the female body from an object that bears the mark of trauma within cultural narratives to the active creator of her own testimony?

In chapter 5, the black female body takes on the role of mediator for the testimony of the traumatized black subject and the individual and cultural responses to it. The chapter also explores the forces of technology as they mediate contemporary scenes of suffering. In Anna Deavere Smith's play *Twilight: Los Angeles, 1992*, the city pavement and police Tasers replace the sweatbox as the site of torture, but the site of testimony and official interpretations remains the courtroom. Just as Williams explores and exposes the biased perspective of the supposedly objective historian through the character of Nehemiah, Anna Deavere Smith challenges the evidence presented in the Simi Valley courtroom in which the officers who beat Rodney King were tried. The chapter focuses on issues of testimony and the visual realm, including video and media technology that rapidly reproduces the image of the violated body while silencing the survivor's voice. Anna Deavere Smith places the video image on pause, and through the community of voices that she creates in her performance and play, she lingers in a twilight of meaning, an unsettled space that acknowledges the belatedness of traumatic experience and the possibilities of community testimony.

1 / "The Quick Gasp of Sympathy":
Trauma and Interracial Witnessing in
Sherley Anne Williams's *Dessa Rose*

"Memory stopped" for Dessa, the protagonist of Sherley Anne Williams's *Dessa Rose*, which opens with an imprisoned female slave recounting in "halting speech and hesitant manner" her experience in a recent slave rebellion.[1] Ashraf Rushdy describes the novel as a neoslave narrative, "a particular form of the contemporary narrativity of slavery" influenced by the cultural politics of the late 1960s, when, he asserts, "the study of American slavery was invigorated by a renewed respect for the truth and value of slave testimony, the significance of slave cultures, and the importance of slave resistance."[2] The event linked to this "death" in Dessa's memory happened the day she faced the dead body of her beloved, Kaine, who died during the slave rebellion, which has occurred before the novel begins. This death of memory marks the site of trauma.

The point at which "memory stopped" is crucial to the understanding of the novel's representation of traumatic experience. Imprisoned in body and mind at the novel's opening and forced to meet with a writer who interrogates her about the slave rebellion, Dessa finds herself drawn to the traumatic event: "Dessa came back to that moment again and again, recognizing it as dead, knowing there was no way to change it, arriving at it from various directions, refusing to move beyond it. Out there was nightmare, Kaine's body, cold and clammy beneath her hands, Master laughing in her face, the horror that scarred her inner thighs, snaking around her lower abdomen and hips in ropy keloids that gleamed with patent-leather smoothness."[3] The moment has lost its fluidity, its ability to change with Dessa as she continues to move through time in the present. It remains fixed and silent beneath her consciousness, and the novel's narrative, circling around the moment, reflects this gap.

The evidence of the moment exists outside narrative. Dessa's lips remain locked in silence, however, in part because the meaning of the events has been evacuated from her memory. She keeps images of the moments leading up to the death of Kaine and the sweatbox, the torture device in which she was enclosed for an extended period in her own waste, but the content of the images remains unchanged in their relentless repetition. Divorced from emotions, the images record the scene in the past with precise detail while eliding the element of suffering. Clearly intended to break her spirit, the sweatbox in fact fractures her memory. She survives the experience through unconscious separation from it. Her body bears the scars that speak to the relationship between trauma and the body, and what is lost in narrative is always present, inescapably, indelibly imprinted in the body. The scars, which Mae Henderson describes as "inscriptions [that] produce the meaning of black female subjectivity in the discursive domain of slavery,"[4] form a text that multiple readers must negotiate, including Dessa herself. This break between the kind of memory that can be recalled in language and image and the kind that can only be sensed by the body has been identified as a defining feature of traumatic response. For Dessa, the break in memory, the point of rupture in language, occurs across her genitals. The connection between her sexuality and the suppression of her memory is difficult to ignore. Kobena Mercer posits, "Sexuality is a front-line point of access to the colonised psyche."[5] The scarring marks an attempt to write over Dessa's access to the power and pleasure of her own body, to inscribe the law of racial ideology, and to erase violently her desire to claim her life as her own. She is silenced not only within the public sphere but also within her own body. Her ability to connect, to communicate on a most intimate level with another human being, has been hindered both physically and psychically. By brutally damaging her genitals during her pregnancy, the slave master threatens to alter the association between the love she received from Kaine and the child that will pass through her in birth.

Dessa's audience, the white writer Nehemiah, tries to negotiate the discrepancy between her confused presentation and the violent acts of which she has been accused. Beginning with the violated body of Dessa Rose, an imprisoned slave, the narrative reveals the desire to constrict and contain the possible signification of her body, even in relation to her own story. The text deals with the production of an official narrative that refuses to recognize survivor testimony, mirroring the original violation threatening to annihilate the survivor's voice. The story told is one of interpretation and reception, of readings and misreadings based on the identities inscribed on survivors' bodies within a racist cultural code. It interrogates the spectacle of the racialized body, to question how seeing detracts from listening and impedes testimony. The novel reveals the gaps in sight, the shock evoked by images that transgress the rigid binary of black and white, and ultimately suggests possibilities for moving beyond the spectacle of racial difference into a realm of empathy.

The deep connections between social context and testimony that the novel implies allow for the exploration of the listener's integral role in understanding the crisis. By placing emphasis on the position of the receiver, we can see cultural constructions of racial difference interfering with the way we receive evidence and acknowledge violence done to bodies of racialized or gendered others. The ending of *Dessa Rose* suggests the possibility of creating a space in which body and voice can unite to speak experience and be heard, where the survivor's story penetrates the witness, breaking the seal that separates self and other.

"The absence of an empathetic listener," Dori Laub suggests, "or more radically, the absence of an addressable other, an other who can hear the anguish of one's memories and thus affirm and recognize their realness, annihilates the story."[6] Since Nehemiah comes to the encounter with a predetermined understanding of Dessa as inferior in both gender and race, a belief that he seeks only to confirm through the meeting and to advance within his writing, he cannot serve as a reliable witness or as Laub's "addressable other." Dessa does not intentionally withhold the details of her worst hour from herself or others. In complete isolation, she does not have access to the memories that would form her story. She only has the physical evidence, her scars, to remind her that something has happened to her. A brief description of her days after the rebellion from the coffle, provided by the third-person narrator, signals this gap in memory: "Even when others spoke around the campfire, during the days of their freedom, about their trials under slavery, Dessa was silent. Their telling awoke no echoes in her mind. That part of the past lay sealed in the scars between her thighs."[7] Her most brutal memories remain trapped within her body. Judith Herman, in her groundbreaking analysis, describes the necessity for survivors to transcend the boundaries that limit their understanding of the traumatic experience and its implications for the present.[8] This process entails creating a dynamic space in which the survivor finds multiple readings of the experience to combat the relentless repetition of a single memory.

Recent scholarship on race has focused on decentering whiteness and on making apparent the constructedness of white racial identity. Cultural critic Ruth Frankenberg argues in her essay "When We Are Capable of Stopping, We Begin to See" that whiteness as an identity relies on the enactment of particular behaviors that become naturalized through repetition: "I have been performing whiteness, and having whiteness performed upon me since—or actually before—the moment I was born."[9] In *Dessa Rose*, Nehemiah and Rufel, the white woman occupying the abandoned plantation where the escaped slaves hide, perform or enact whiteness in ways that become apparent in their specific and complex responses to Dessa as a survivor. Just as Dori Laub contends, the testimony exposes the receiver as well as the survivor. In this case, their reactions to Dessa, their interpretations of her scars and her words, prove their position within the racist scheme that tries to undo her. Through their interactions with Dessa, they must face themselves and make a choice. They must decide between continuing to act as perpetrators by failing to recognize Dessa's testimony and resisting the identification with whiteness and the racial fictions that deny black subjectivity.

Susan Stanford Friedman describes "scripts of relational positionality ... [that] regard identity as situationally constructed and defined at the crossroads of different systems of alterity and stratification."[10] Relational positionality acknowledges the multiple forces at work in the manifestation of identity. "Scripts of relational positionality" contest a fixed reading that denies the effect of context, cultural conditioning, and the fluidity of individual relationships. Their textuality resists binaries, such as black/white and male/female, that allow individuals to remain defined according to an oppositional structure that privileges one term at the expense of the other. The initial script of post-traumatic experience relies on this kind of binary structure. The traumatic memory remains beyond the survivor's grasp, its meaning locking the survivor in a rigid dichotomy of victim/perpetrator. Relational positionality can be compared to the movement away from this fixity, when the survivor creates a new, dynamic relationship between the self in memory and in the present. *Dessa Rose* provides examples of these two types of scripts, particularly in relation to the process of making meaning from a traumatic experience. These scripts allow insight into the psyches of the individuals who participate in their construction, giving the opportunity to hear from survivors of racism's violence and to respond to the writer Toni Morrison's call "to see what racial ideology does to the mind, imagination, and behavior of masters."[11] In the novel's early scenes with Nehemiah and Dessa, the code of racial ideology determines the relationship between them. Dessa's story and the memory that informs it, therefore, remain trapped; only one possible reading exists based on her position within the racial binary. Later, after the rebellion and Dessa's interrogation, when Dessa returns to the abandoned plantation, a border space between past and present worlds, the complexities of her story emerge.

In the novel's first section, Nehemiah and the white male court define her scars as a mark of insubordination and beastliness. Within this context, the scars remain a source of pain and shame for Dessa, and although she faces their constant reminder of her pain, her conscious mind protects her from piecing together the incident that created this brutal legacy. Thus, the context and her audience seem to hinder her ability to remember and to establish a psychic space in which her pain can create its own language.

The first page of the novel introduces the reader to a brief time line of the events that have led to Dessa's imprisonment. Nehemiah creates this strictly factual list and desires to flesh out the details through his interactions with Dessa, the subject of his research. He regards Dessa as an opportunity to advance the cause of his most recent project, a book on managing rebellious slaves, to follow his successful first book, *The Master's Complete Guide to Dealing with Slaves and Other Dependents*. Despite his persistence, however, he finds the task of moving from his sketchy rendering to a more complete portrait nearly impossible. The missing component is Dessa's memory. He attributes her silence to ignorance or insolence. Failing to understand the consequences of such an extreme experience on the memory of its survivor, he believes that a program of deprivation, threats, and manipulation will force the story from her closed lips.

Dessa struggles to find words to describe her recent experiences. She relies on images and sensory memories, telling the story from a survivor's perspective. Meaning cannot be extracted through simple narration of facts. Laurence Kirmayer suggests, "Traumatic experience is not a story but a cascade of experiences, eruptions, crevasses, a sliding of tectonic plates that undergird the self. These disruptions then give rise to an effort to interpret and so to smooth, stabilize, recalibrate."[12] During

Dessa's imprisonment, she lives through the constant "disruption" in her psychic life following trauma. Her struggle to know her experience occurs on multiple levels. The memories of her previous life flood the dark, damp space, grounded in the soil of death and rebirth. The bodily nature of memory becomes tangible as Dessa moves across the floor of her cell: "Always, whether her eyes were open or closed, Kaine walked with her, or mammy. Jeeter tugged at her head-rag or Carrie Mae Lefonia, Martha—They sat with her in the cellar. She grieved in this presence as she had not done since their loss."[13] Through memory, she creates a space in which her body and soul, even for a fleeting moment, can feel its former connection to community and intimacy: "Dessa flowered briefly, fled in dry spasm, gone suddenly as the dream had come, so lifelike had she felt herself with him, knew herself among Carrie and them, been swept up in the warmth of their presence."[14]

Although Dessa's body relives moments of love by raising memories, she appears to have lost the bodily link to the horror of the events that follow Kaine's death. Nehemiah describes her lack of affect when talking about the violence through which she recently lived: "It had been an entrancing recital, better in its way than a paid theatrical . . . all narrated with about as much expression as one gave to a 'Howdy' with any passing stranger."[15] The flatness of Dessa's narration reveals more about her condition than Nehemiah has the capacity to recognize. It is precisely at the point of this flatness that the most powerful experience has been embedded. Roberta Culbertson describes the detachment of memory's emotional component from the factual recounting of the survivor's past: "The one who speaks without emotion presents only what [Charlotte] Delbo calls an 'external' memory—socially constructed, skating along the surfaces of words and engaging the intellect—not the body's reexperience, which because it is a recapitulation of the past, cannot be spoken about or related at the moment, just as it could not be originally. It is not known in words, but in the body."[16] However, Nehemiah dismisses Dessa's failure to display feelings. For him, it signals her bestial status. Within his racist worldview, Dessa does not possess a moral compass to guide her actions or responses.

Before and during the telling of her story, Dessa faces efforts to control the meaning of the events leading to her imprisonment. Dessa's testimony does not conform to Nehemiah's expectations and desire. Failing to see her as a human who has just suffered extreme trauma, he reacts with doubt and confusion to her attempts to present her story:

> There had been nothing in the darky's halting speech and hesitant manner to suggest the slave revolt leader she was convicted of being. Held spellbound by that very discrepancy, Adam Nehemiah had leaned forward from his perch on the cellar steps the better to hear the quiet rasp of her voice. He hadn't caught every word; often he had puzzled overlong at some unfamiliar idiom or phrase, now and then losing the tale in the welter of names the darky called. Or he had sat, fascinated, forgetting to write. Yet the scene was vivid in his mind as he deciphered the darky's account from his hastily scratched notes and he reconstructed it in his journal as though he remembered it word for word.[17]

The "halting speech" with its gaps and uncertainties fits within the realm of probable responses to trauma, when "language is in process and in trial,"[18] but this connection to deeper truths is quickly overwritten by Nehemiah's hand.

Unable to tolerate the ambiguity that threatens to alter his relation to Dessa, Nehemiah seals the scene with his own words, fitting her story within his own. She provides him with an opportunity to demonstrate his expertise to the wealthy southern slaveholders. Her story will allow him into a world he has existed on the fringes of his entire life. He signifies authority, the experts who are in the position to record events, impressions, and history. Through his character, we see the construction of an official story, one that uses the facts of the event to serve its own end. She must escape not only from slavery itself but also from the legacy of the brutal institution, from the desire to own not only her body but also her story: to tell it, record it, interpret it so that it meets the needs of the dominant culture. Nehemiah's preconceptions about slaves lead him to react incredulously to the information he receives from Dessa. For example, he cannot fathom that slaves practiced birth control and abortion to thwart "breeding" efforts of the slaveholders. His repeated questioning about the file that he believes must have been part of the escape from the coffle often disrupts Dessa's speech, causing her to shut down in silence.

Nehemiah's response to Dessa's body signals his inability to identify with her as a human being. He finds her repulsive and compares her jail cell to an animal's den, where she sits on her "haunches." Through Nehemiah's reaction to Dessa, Williams exposes a subjectivity completely informed by a racial ideology. At every moment of their interaction, he positions himself as superior in relation to Dessa. He is made in direct relation to her unmaking. In the close space, he fears contamination: "He sniffed gingerly at his sleeve now, but could detect no telltale odor. Really, he must speak to Hughes about making provision for another meeting place. Being closeted with the darky within the small confines of the cellar was an unsettling experience."[19] He worries that he will become infected by her body, not only that he will carry her smell away with him but that the difference between them has narrowed and that his whiteness has been corrupted by her blackness.

At the end of the novel, Dessa finds herself faced with the same man who tried to violate her in language, and she is forced to return to the most painful moments of her life. Nehemiah wants her to strip naked in front of male authorities, to display her wounds as evidence of her guilt. By this time, however, the scars that lie across her genitals are no longer proof of her wild, untamed nature. They cannot be used as that kind of evidence, suggesting a transformation in the symbolic value of the scars. The difference is in Dessa's relationship with other women. When the women see the damage done to her body, they do not blame her. A transformation occurs between these two scenes. The transformation involves Dessa and Rufel, the white woman who has been abandoned by her husband on a dilapidated plantation.

In *Give Birth to Brightness*, Sherley Anne Williams's 1972 critical analysis of what she refers to as "neo-black literature," Williams writes, "As the object of an almost always illicit desire and the butt of ribald, taunting jokes, the white woman is one of the most traditional figures in the culture and history of Black people in America."[20] In the tradition that Williams describes, the white woman has no redeeming qualities. She is selfish, childish, and mean, calculating and manipulative, using her femininity and her status as the unattainable sexual object to undermine black masculinity. In *Dessa Rose*, white womanhood is a menacing, haunting presence that must be confronted, demystified, and transcended. Through the character of Rufel, whose position within society has been shattered when her husband abandons her, the sanctity of white womanhood becomes corrupted. She is transformed from the belle of the land, an image she can only resurrect in memory, to "Miz Ruint." In this case, her "ruin" takes on positive connotations because it is the deconstruction of white womanhood as defined in relation to its "purity" or separation from blackness.

The destruction of Rufel as the emblem of white womanhood occurs as Dessa emerges from her traumatic unmaking and begins the process of reconstitution. There is a connection between the two women that warrants further exploration. As their relationship progresses, their struggle to define themselves in relation to and away from each other becomes the force that pushes the narrative forward. Evelynn Hammonds describes the relationship between black and white womanhood in a racist culture: "there is the way black women's sexuality has been constructed in a binary opposition to that of white women: it is rendered simultaneously invisible, visible (exposed), hypervisible, and pathologized in dominant discourses."[21] As Dessa emerges from her trauma to claim her own survival and story, she participates in the creation of a narrative that rebuilds her psyche through the destruction of the binary defining black and white women.

In Dessa's previous life as a field servant, she had very little exposure to white women. She did, however, have one encounter that changed her life forever:

> Once the white man's questioning had driven her into that desert and Young Mistress had risen from the waste, clothes torn, hair screaming, red-faced, red-mouthed. The four red welts in the suddenly pallid face, the white spot where the thumb had pressed the base of the red neck filled Dessa with a terror and glee so intense they were almost physical. Frightened at her own response, she was almost ashamed—not of the deed. No. Never that, but surely it was wrong to delight so deeply in anyone else's pain. She had seen the blood and bits of pink flesh beneath her own fingernails, felt the loose skin of Young Mistress's neck. And clamped her mouth shut, clanked her arms across her chest. She should have killed the white woman; they would have killed her then. It would have all been over; none of this would have begun.[22]

For Dessa, the image of a battered white woman marks the beginning of her painful journey, and her violent encounter with "Young Mistress" after the death of her beloved Kaine has altered her physical and emotional landscape. She finds herself left with an ambivalence toward her actions and the emotions they evoke. Psychic pain returns in the form of embodied memory when she encounters another white woman, Rufel, after her rescue from the jail. According to trauma experts such as Judith Herman and Bessel van der Kolk, the emotional and physical responses of the original experience are raised when the survivor perceives a potential threat in a new situation. Dessa awakens to Rufel's presence before she has an opportunity to come to terms with her survival from the threat of execution. The initial scene in which Dessa feels the shock of seeing Rufel so close to her marks the beginning of a series of moments, of shocking scenes, that alter the dynamic between the visual field of evidence and cross-racial witnessing.

The plantation functions as an open, unfinished space, in opposition to the jailhouse, and its inhabitants undergo change in this unsettled realm. It has been abandoned by its owner, Rufel's husband, and the slaves who once worked its land. In the center of the house, a staircase leads to nowhere, the result of an incomplete expansion project. No one has checked on Rufel and her children. She has been left in ruin, to degenerate with the walls around her. Like an underwater shipwreck, the house seems to blur the boundaries between the artificial and the organic as it becomes consumed by its natural surroundings. It moves from a work in progress with a structural plan devised in strict accordance with societal norms to a textual site whose meaning and function change according to the desires and needs of its current occupants. As a site of memory and loss, it allows these occupants to linger in its ambiguity long enough for traumatic memory to sift through its multiple layers of meaning without becoming set in a single interpretation. For the fugitive slaves and Rufel, the degeneration of the plantation and the world it represented allows for a transformation in identity. The structure no longer holds, and neither do the identities once fixed within it.

Four scenes set on the plantation disrupt the violence of Dessa's original encounter with Young Mistress, for which the desired outcome was the death of both women, black and white. Each scene involves witnessing across difference, particularly in relation to the female body, maternity, and sexuality. These scenes depict the change in the women's relationship to each other and their sense of their own identity as women. The scenes lead them into an ability to serve as true witnesses to each other as survivors. They allow the women to know the other's struggle on multiple levels: emotionally, intellectually, and bodily and as mothers, daughters, lovers, and finally, as friends. The categories of difference that construct black and white womanhood in opposition to each other and prevent witnessing are broken down through empathy. The women's encounter forces them to confront their own demons, reflected in their initial reaction to each other's story of survival and means of coping with the struggles in their lives.

Dessa awakens from her sleep and asks for her baby, Desmond. What she sees is this: "The white woman, her shoulder still bare, the curly black head and brown face of a new baby nestled at her breast, faced her now. 'See?'"[23] Dessa cannot fathom the possibility that maternal concern crosses racial boundaries. Nothing in her experience allows for such a possibility. Her reaction confirms the terror the scene evokes for her: "'Naaaaaawwwww!' The scream rushed out of her on an explosion of breath. She saw the glass-colored eyes buck before her own squeezed tight. The covers weighed her arms and legs; some voice screamed, 'Annabelle. Annabelle, get Ada! She starting up again!'"[24]

Faced with the sight of her child in the arms of the enemy, Dessa fears the final possession of her soul. For Dessa the sight raises feelings of violation, a revisitation with the most traumatic moment of her life. She awakes to see the only piece of Kaine she has left being swallowed by horrifying whiteness. The reader is aware that Rufel means no harm to the baby. Dessa, however, is startled by the appropriation of the mothering role.

In spite of Dessa's initial shock, this scene introduces the white woman's role in her recovery. The violence, it seems, has caused Dessa's milk to dry up. The white woman becomes a surrogate for her, nurturing her child while she heals. This moment signals a shift from Dessa as violated body to healing spirit. She is faced with the enemy, the pain that the white female body evokes, and experiences the transformation of that pain. This is not to suggest that Rufel's role in this recovery is intentional or based in her own goodwill. She enters into a process of discovery as well. Her attitude toward Dessa, whom she often refers to as "the wench," is at first not much different from Nehemiah's attitude. The critical difference between Rufel and Nehemiah occurs on a bodily level of empathy. Rufel responds physically to Dessa's suffering and the newborn's needs.

Rufel's act of nursing Dessa's baby shocks not only Dessa but all the refugees hiding at the plantation, including Ada and Harker: "No one would ever know, she had assured herself, and feeling the feeble tug at her nipple, he's hungry and only a baby. Lulled as she was by the gentle rhythm and spent by the drama of the morning's events, she had dozed—and awakened to the startled faces of Ada and Harker. Their consternation had been almost comic. Ada had stuttered and Harker had gaped. In the pause Rufel had recovered her own composure, feeling somehow vindicated in her actions by their very confusion. She had confounded them—rendered Ada speechless."[25] In this scene, the image shocks. The image of a white breast and a black mouth suggests a startling relationship, an unfathomable intimacy. It marks the beginning of the emergence of "Miz Ruint." Whether or not Rufel's motivation may strike some readers as essentialist, Williams's Rufel makes her decision to nurse Dessa's baby based on an instinct or drive to protect the help-less infant. One could argue that she is simply fighting two strands of cultural indoctrination. The first involves her role as mother. The second relates to her concern about appearances as a white woman. Her feeling of shame upon being discovered reveals her internalization of the white-supremacist ideology of her time. Either way, it becomes clear that the former strand wins the struggle.

The response to Rufel's act of surrogate mothering establishes what Marta Sanchez refers to as "the geographical and psychologi-cal space . . . [that] marks a cultural borderlands where a marginalized white woman and a female slave fugitive encounter each other."[26] The encounter that this space allows problematizes components of gender and ethnic identity that have been naturalized in the dominant sphere.

As Rufel sits by Dessa's bed, she relives the glory of her former life in an incantation of memory. Unable to decipher Rufel's speech, Dessa be-lieves that Rufel suffers from delusions. Dessa does recognize a repeated reference to "Mammy." Rufel's references allude to Dorcas, a servant pur-chased by her father as a childhood birthday gift. The white woman's love for the deceased caregiver remains fixed at the level of childhood. Rufel loved the way Dorcas cared for her. Even in memory, "Mammy" provides sustenance for Rufel's fledgling ego, as she feeds on the dead woman's image. The psychic dimensions of their relationship bear a resemblance to Virginia Woolf's well-known metaphor comparing women to mirrors that enhance the male reflection but receive no reciprocal magnification. Dorcas made Rufel beautiful dresses, told her she possessed a certain beauty, and listened to her recount in great detail every social engage-ment. And Rufel accepted, even demanded, this treatment like a small child who expects her mother to live for her alone.

When Dessa can no longer tolerate Rufel's erasure of Dorcas's identi-ty, she invokes memories of her own biological mother, which reveal the constraints on black motherhood under slavery. At the very moment she is disrupting Rufel's naive ideas about her relationship to Dorcas, Dessa also exposes slavery's brutally hypocritical treatment of motherhood. Dessa forces Rufel to see a distinction between "Mammy" as a cultural fiction, an identity created by the complete denial of black female subjec-tivity, and the real woman who did not have any choice but to provide care for this white child.

Language and the ability to determine the meaning of history belong to Dessa in this scene. Overwhelmed by the need to voice the previously unspoken details of her own mother's life, Dessa performs a testimony of naming that implicates her listener, Rufel, in the crime of erasing the individual identity of Dorcas, the woman she has known only as "Mammy" from her youth. Toni Morrison's call for a focus on the individuals who benefit from racism and the impact of this benefit on their subjectivity is answered in the interaction between the two women. When Dessa seizes the scene to tell the story of her mother's strength and loss, she causes Rufel to acknowledge her own blindness, however desperately she fights it. It is Rufel who is exposed, even though Dessa discloses the depth of her grief over her mother's pain.

Rufel does not willingly submit to this transformation in consciousness. Instead, she desperately seeks to undermine Dessa, particularly as one who testifies to painful truths from which Rufel has been sheltered her entire life. In Rufel's search for evidence to discredit Dessa's voice, she targets Dessa's greatest vulnerability, the trauma involving her scars. Rufel learns about Dessa's scars from Nathan, a leader within the group of escaped slaves, and her initial reaction mixes disbelief and horror: "Rufel could see the scene as he described it. The darky himself tying the wench's hands, looping the lead rope over the pommel of his saddle, walking the horse across the yard and around to the front of the house as she stumbled along behind, seeing the darkies lining the drive, some as he said, hiding their faces, others staring straight ahead. Had her own people been there, Rufel wondered, her own Rose? She could almost feel the fire that must have lived in the wench's thighs."[27] The violence becomes tangible to Rufel in that moment. She comes close to living it as it engages her sense of sight, sound, and touch. Yet even after hearing Nathan and Dessa's story about life in slavery, she finds "it hard to reconcile" her memories with the living bodies before her. What appears to be most difficult for her to come to terms with is the possibility that "her own people" take part daily in the brutal system of slavery. At each moment of witnessing, Rufel must confront her own complicity. For Rufel, this complicity translates mostly into willful ignorance. She had asked her husband not to whip slaves in the yard. Standing with Nathan, she wonders if he had simply moved the whippings to the woods, where screams could not be heard from the house.

As her own position within the system of slavery becomes difficult to ignore, she seeks safety in finding just cause for Dessa's pain. "She must have done something pretty bad," Rufel contends, although she is "unable herself to imagine such a crime."[28] She attempts to excuse Dessa's former mistress by relying on stereotypes about black female sexuality that would figure Dessa as a seductress of white men. Nathan quickly disproves this accusation and exposes Rufel's pettiness for needing visual proof, to see Dessa's scars, before she believes her story. In Rufel's search for validation of her own life, she must face the truth that Dessa represents. Through her relationship with Dessa, Rufel undergoes a radical transformation in her identity as a white woman.

Rufel becomes obsessed with discrediting Dessa's story. An unwilling witness, Rufel wants to annihilate the story. In one unexpected moment, however, her desire to escape is violently thwarted. Immersed in her own thoughts, she opens the door to the bedroom and finds Dessa standing nude. For one instant, the shock of facing Dessa's scars overwhelms her ability to deny the violence of slavery: "Barely able to suppress the quick gasp of sympathy surprised from her by that glimpse of the dark body, and acutely embarrassed, Rufel closed the door. The wench's loins looked like a mutilated cat face. Scar tissue plowed through her pubic region so no hair would ever grow there again. Rufel leaned weakly against the door, regretting what she had seen. The wench had a right to hide her scars, her pain."[29]

Distressed at what she has just witnessed, Rufel must acknowledge that Dessa's scars, and the story they tell, belong to her. The scars serve as text inscribing the violence of racism over the black female body, her sexual autonomy, and her ability to reproduce. As an extreme text, these inscriptions compel readings that force their audience to own or disown a position in relation to the ideology marking her body and thwarting its efforts to write its own meaning, trapped in a permanent childlike state of dependence symbolized by the impeded growth of pubic hair. Her body, once viewed as public property available to any white person's proprietary gaze, becomes her own, finally "private" in Rufel's sight. To gaze at Dessa's scars without her knowledge signifies another violation, another attempt to steal Dessa's control over her own body, its physical and psychic meaning, and it would appear that Rufel recognizes this violation, feeling ashamed at her own behavior.

Unknowingly, Rufel's search leads her to discredit her own ideas about black female sexuality. Following this narrative sequence, Williams destabilizes the construction of white female sexuality through characters' testimony and a scene that shocks the characters into facing that which they previously thought inconceivable. When the group finds Rufel and Nathan in bed together, they can only manage a "startled gasp" and the words "Mis—Nathan!"[30] Nathan's history provides a glimpse into the constraints placed on white female sexuality in the nineteenth century. Miz Lorraine, his former mistress who used her power over male slaves to satisfy her sexual needs, would have been considered a freak if she had expressed her sexuality openly or with a white man:

> Nature was strong in her; she did not call on him that often, no more than once or twice every month or so, but when she did, she kept him awake most of the night and sometimes kept him for a day or even two. If she had tried to satisfy her sexual needs with white men, even ones outside her own class, she would have had no way of ensuring their silence. If a black man boasted, she could have his life. He never learned who else, if anyone, besides her maid knew of the mistress's habits. He talked to no one about what he did and no one talked to him. This is what Miz Lorraine wanted: to be in control.[31]

The relationship between Nathan and Miz Lorraine reveals a complex dynamic of abuse and desire. The situation proves the falseness of white femininity, how it constrains and denies essential elements of subjectivity, and the power that even the weakest member of white society had over black slaves. It also makes clear the desire that always accompanies abuse of power. Miz Lorraine, therefore, is exposed in a scene of her own creation, and Nathan comes away with more knowledge of the struggles in her soul than she would have ever intended.

Dessa reacts with outrage to the sight of Rufel and Nathan in bed together. She feels betrayed by Nathan, and his lust disgusts her. The man most deeply associated with her liberation has surrendered to a white woman, the enemy who threatened her bodily and psychic integrity.

Before the novel begins, Dessa was whipped after she slapped her former mistress for insinuating that the plantation master had fathered the baby she carried. With that accusation, the mistress denied Dessa's connection to Kaine, the man she loved and lost to white violence. Her punishment, again, sought to control, if not destroy, her sexuality.

The scene with Rufel and Nathan awakens a sense of searching in Dessa and provides Harker with an opportunity to reveal his feelings for her. When Rufel demands that Dessa apologize for calling her "Miz Ruint" and threatens to thwart Harker's plan, Dessa refuses and expresses her contempt for any plan that requires trusting a white woman. An argument ensues, and one of the men, Ned, calls the black women "mules" who are jealous of Nathan's relationship with Rufel. The attack leaves Dessa shaking with rage: "And then there was silence. Silence and a fire-burst where Ned's head should've been when I looked at him. I had to close my eyes. Was this what they thought of us? Mules. I was so choked I couldn't speak."[32] She thinks of the damage done to each woman in the room, their bodies used to breed and to please someone else's desire. And she thinks of Kaine and wonders, "Had he really wanted me to be like Mistress . . . like Miz Ruint, that doughy skin and slippery hair?"[33]

The white woman's value as a desirable object correlates directly to Dessa's feelings of shame about her brutalized body. When Harker tells her that her scars only intensify his desire for her, he assigns high value to her status as a rebel and a survivor. The white woman's unmarked skin exposes her privileged life and her lack of struggle, but it also reveals her status as a well-kept possession. Dessa's scars are read as a sign of her subjectivity reaching beyond the boundaries of property toward self-possession, despite the dear price paid for such an assertion.

This reading of her scars against Rufel's "doughy skin," and the desire it suggests, elicits an emotional response that raises the memory of the sweatbox. For the first time in the narrative, Dessa remembers the life-time of moments she spent trapped in the enclosed space: "I had cried for a long time in that box, from pain, from grief, from filth. That filth, my filth. You know, this do something to you. To have to lay up in filth. You not a baby—baby have clean skin, clean mind. He think his shit is interesting; he want to show it to you. But you know this dirt. Laying up in my own foulment made me know how low I was. And I cried. I was like an animal; whipped like one; in dirt like one. I had never known people could do peoples like this. And I had the marks of that on my privates."[34] The point at which "memory stopped" opens up when Dessa must face her own sexuality after seeing Nathan and Rufel's coupling and learning about Harker's attraction to her. She has to deal with not only the anger at what she had been denied, which Rufel's unmarked body evokes, but also the startling possibility that, even after the defilement of her "privates," someone could still find her worth loving. The realization that she "had never known people could do peoples like this" proves that the incident shocked her psyche, moving well beyond her previous exposure to the human potential for cruelty. That shock created the gap in memory, a gap that could only be traversed with the force of another shock, which returned her to the point at which the memory was sealed.

Farah Griffin argues in her discussion of the "textual healing" and "the erotic as a foundation for resistance" that "heterosexuality acts as a plot catalyst to action and as a narrative resolution throughout Williams' novel."[35] At one level, this argument appears to be viable because Nathan and Rufel's relationship and Harker's disclosure of his desire causes Dessa to process her most painful memories. However, it does not seem that the novel relies on heterosexuality alone as a liberating or healing force. Heterosexuality acts as a plot catalyst only when it evokes the trauma that Dessa has undergone on a bodily and psychic level, and the scene between Rufel and Nathan, which arouses confusion, anger, and pain in Dessa, is only one of several scenes involving Rufel and Dessa that function in the same manner. Within these scenes, the naked body of the other woman produces an identification with sameness that threatens the difference on which racism depends. Desmond nursing at Rufel's breast forces Dessa to confront and to survive the appropriation of her own body and ability to mother under slavery. The entwined bodies of Rufel and Nathan raise up the pain of her loss of Kaine, their profound love for each other, and the scars she bears that threaten her sexuality. Rufel too receives a transformative shock when she encounters the scars across Dessa's "privates" and, closing the door, finally sees Dessa as a woman who has a right to her own body. The visible in these scenes defies the "evidence" of the early scenes with Nehemiah. In these cases, believing does not inform and produce seeing; rather, seeing destroys previous beliefs.

In a final scene of witnessing between the two women, Rufel's vulnerability—and not her sexual agency—challenges Dessa's perception of power within the dominant order. This challenge occurs when the group stops for the night at a plantation owned by a man referred to as "Mr. Oscar." Still posing as a wife traveling the countryside to sell slaves for her family, Rufel receives the expected gestures of hospitality from Mr. Oscar. She performs her role as southern lady, eating, drinking, and socializing with her gentleman host. Dessa believes that Rufel enjoys the role-playing a bit too much and watches the white woman carefully for any mistakes that she should report to Harker. It seems that Rufel is reveling in the privilege that her whiteness allows, even if she now acknowledges the identity as fictional.

During that night, Dessa awakens to noises coming from Rufel and Mr. Oscar in Rufel's bed. Although she immediately assumes that the white woman has invited the man to her bed, she soon realizes that Rufel is involved in a struggle with the drunken man. After the two women manage to push Mr. Oscar from the room, they try to get some rest in the bed that only minutes before held the threatening figure. Dessa remains startled by the potential violation: "I laid awake a long time that night while she snored quiet on the other side of the baby. The white woman was subject to the same ravishment as me; this thought kept me awake. I hadn't knowed white mens could use a white woman like that, just take her by force same as they could with us."[36]

This reflection marks a key moment in Dessa's healing. Her realization of white women's vulnerability allows her to connect with Rufel as an individual woman. When Dessa considers white women's potential for violation, she confronts the weakness of the another woman, the white mistress who ordered her whippings, who haunts her worst moments and represents in her memory, more than any other, the breaking point in her psychic life. I am not arguing that she forgives or even understands this white woman's previous cruelty. However, in this scene Dessa's realization that white women's power has limits in the world would seem to alter their threatening presence within her inner life.

Representations of whiteness, bell hooks suggests, often reflect "the traumatic pain and anguish that remain a consequence of white racist domination, a psychic state that informs and shapes the way black folks 'see' whiteness."[37] In *Dessa Rose*, there is a shift from the black body as a site of trauma and a sight to be controlled within the white gaze to an emphasis on "seeing" whiteness and the institutions dominated by white-supremacist beliefs. Through the perspectives of Dessa, Nathan, and Harker, the black gaze and voice gain control of the scene, and white inhumanity becomes the spectacle. In this way, survivors recognize the limitations of the perpetrators of horrible, institutionalized violence.

The group's scheme to trick the white slave buyers involves a performance that denaturalizes the conditions and relationships buttressing the institution of slavery. In the plan, Rufel acts as a plantation mistress who needs to sell slaves because her family has fallen on hard times. Traveling from town to town and changing their story along the way, the "slaves" are sold only to escape, meet the group, and begin the process all over again.

In the group's intentional reenactment of the traumatic conditions of slavery, they become more conscious of the pain evoked by the life they had once known. They relive memories and take risks, but importantly, this repetition includes their ability to claim their own survival. Cathy Caruth's claim that trauma is "locatable not in one moment alone but in the relation between two moments"[38] is reflected in Dessa's painful awakening. She becomes her own witness, seeing and feeling the brutality to which she has been subjected as if for the first time. When Dessa stands before the auction block and watches as the white auctioneer pinches and prods her friend, overhearing the comments made by spectators about the bargains to be had on this occasion, she becomes overwhelmed by the horrible knowledge this scene provides. She encounters the betrayal of her own flesh through the body of another. Pain that left her numb, her speech flat, and her memory broken, a trauma too powerful to face, emerges through indirect sight.

Farah Griffin describes Sherley Anne Williams as belonging to a group of African American women writers who "replace the dominant discourse's obsession with the visual black body with a perspective that privileges touch and other senses."[39] Dessa's journey brings her face to face with the man who would use the marks of her suffering against her. When Nehemiah finds Dessa in the town center without Rufel, he recognizes her immediately. Her image has been imprinted in his mind as one he had to own. After she is dragged into the sheriff's office, Nehemiah once again tries to rely on the visual "evidence" of her scars to prove that she is the Dessa he seeks. The sheriff sends in an old blind slave to determine the accuracy of Nehemiah's accusations. With one gentle touch, the older woman disrupts the primacy of the visual field. Her ability to feel and to know the meaning of Dessa's scars creates a new reading, one that bears witness to suffering without condemning the survivor to silence. Dessa's story finds its language in that encounter.

The struggle with language and naming that repeats itself throughout the novel always involves naming across difference, or naming the "Other." In the end, Nehemiah's empty pages, which fly from his notebook in the jail, signify the failure of his efforts to seal Dessa's voice and image within his script. Her own narrative, pieced together from a fractured memory, erases his zealous attempts to write her past and present. As she leaves the jail, Dessa corrects Rufel for constantly referring to her as "Odessa" by adding an "O" to her name. She refuses to accept anyone else's version of her reality.

In the novel's epilogue, Dessa's story is told again, but this time she tells it to the children who will know it as part of their own history. Her desire to continue to claim her own story for future generations becomes clear in the novel's final words:

> I hope I live for my people like they do for me, so sharp sometimes I can't believe it's all in my mind. And my mind wanders. This is why I have it all wrote down, why I has the children say it back. I will never forget Nemi trying to read me, knowing I had put myself in his hands. Well this the children have heard from our own lips. I hope they never have to pay what it cost us to own ourselfs. Mother,

brother, sister, husbands, friends . . . my own girlhood all I ever has was the remembrance of a daddy's smile. Oh, we have paid dearly for our children's place in the world again, and again.[40]

In these final words, Dessa remembers the cost of memory. Not only has she freed herself in body, but she has found a language and a narrative to shelter a vulnerable past. This home resides in her young listeners, whose lives bear witness to her survival.

The next chapter discusses another black female body that has left a traumatic legacy for future generations to negotiate. In Suzan-Lori Parks's play *Venus*, a Nehemiah-like figure influenced by Dr. Cuvier, the nineteenth-century French zoologist who dissected the corpse of the Venus Hottentot, tries to "write" her body into his own script of racial hegemony. The Venus, however, must wait over one hundred years before returning to the "children" of her South African home[41] or finding a voice in the Parks play. Later, in chapters 4 and 5, Gayl Jones and Robbie McCauley describe the complexity of being the heirs to these violent legacies.

2 /   Betrayal Trauma and the Test of Complicity in Suzan-Lori Parks's *Venus*

A U.S. Department of Heath and Human Services campaign pamphlet, "Look beneath the Surface," asks health-care providers, "Can you recognize victims of human trafficking among the people you help every day?"[1] The pamphlet then states, "Most victims do not see themselves as victims and do not realize what is being done to them is wrong," a statement that raises complex issues around victim readability and self-awareness. What does it mean to "recognize victims" who "do not see themselves as victims"? As discussed in the preceding chapter, the white writer in *Dessa Rose*, Nehemiah, refuses to recognize Dessa as a victim of horrendous violence because his beliefs about her black body shape his ability to witness the evidence of her trauma. Throughout the novel, Dessa also finds herself unrecognizable in memory around her trauma and the scars that mark her. Like Dessa's initial reluctance to disclose her inner suffering, the DHHS pamphlet refers to trafficked individuals' hesitance to disclose completely upon initial questioning that they are living under conditions that repeatedly traumatize them. They may in fact report the details of their experience, as Dessa does in her flat speech within the jailhouse, but even with this reporting, they do not "see themselves" or "realize what is being done to them is wrong" for reasons not fully explored in the pamphlet.

The pamphlet offers strategies for the health-care worker to read "beneath the surface" presentation—the body—of the possible trafficked woman. In spite of the transparency of the victim's situation in relation to the "clues" described in the pamphlet, she may not be able to read her own situation; she may not recognize herself within the trafficking script. In *Dessa Rose*, Dessa is only able to bear witness to her own suffering after she leaves the hostile environment of the jailhouse, and similar inhibitions may exist for trafficked women.

The pamphlet seems to recommend that care providers disregard the victim's voice here. If the trafficked individual has been questioned about her conditions, and she fails to acknowledge explicitly that she suffers from possible abuse and exploitation, then one can and, the pamphlet implies, should ignore her words. As troubling as this action may seem, it suggests a possible understanding of the complex psychic response to captivity-related, chronic trauma that would alter the victim's self-perception and the possibilities for communicating this sense of experience to others.

In "Law at a Crossroads: The Construction of Migrant Women Trafficked into Prostitution," Nora V. Demleitner identifies another compelling aspect involved in recognizing victims within contemporary trafficking discourse: the spectacle of the violation determines the public response to the victim. As Demleitner puts it, "Much of the reluctance to help trafficked women effectively can be ascribed to the social ambivalence that surrounds their construction as prostitutes and as undocumented migrants."[2] Their marginalized status necessitates graphic displays to overcome the stereotyping: "Only powerful images, such as the forced prostitution of very young girls or brutal forms of physical abuse amounting to torture, have succeeded in overcoming the negative attitude toward prostitutes and 'illegal' immigrants, which is reflected in the reluctant passage and enforcement of antitrafficking laws."[3] As Demleitner suggests, images must meet specific criteria before they elicit an empathetic response within the public imagination. While the public polices the spectacle of the victim's body, the perpetrators remain largely invisible. The *New Statesman* writer Joan Smith argues that "what is becoming clear is that men who use brothels, massage parlours and street prostitutes are the missing link, invisible in most discussions of sex trade."[4] Within contemporary trafficking discourse, the rhetorical burden remains on the individual whose body supplies the services.

Suzan-Lori Parks's play *Venus* addresses the questions about self-awareness, choice, and complicity raised by scholarly and creative responses to human trafficking through her resurrection of Sara Baartman, a.k.a. the Hottentot Venus, who arrived in England from South Africa in

1810. Displayed in London's Piccadilly, Baartman drew crowds interested in having a peak or a poke at her buttocks, which well exceeded European norms. The show caused public stir, with some Londoners accusing her of public indecency and others accusing the showman Cezar of holding Baartman against her will. *Venus* fits well within Parks's oeuvre; her plays return often to the black body violated in contemporary circumstances that reflect, explicitly or implicitly, damaging historical legacies and cultural stereotypes. The Hester character in *In the Blood* and Venus must face public scorn and the projection of blame onto their bodily selves. Both characters have "sin" inscribed on them in public space for activating the illicit desires of the men they encounter. Both characters experience scathing yet flippant judgments for bearing their bodies, presumed guilty in the court of public opinion, and these judgments have direct and devastating consequences for their material existences. As in Parks's other plays *Top Dog/Underdog* and *The Death of the Last Black Man*, cultural stereotypes accompany secret loss and desire and reveal their violent relations to past and present bodies. The Pulitzer-winning Parks appears long concerned with the tremendous psychic cost of the spectacle, the game, or the masquerade and the choices made by characters under their influence.

At the play's center are scenes, influenced by the historical court case, in which Sara Baartman testifies that she remains in England as a free agent. Historically, the case for Baartman's release has links to the abolitionist movement. Mr. M'Cartney, secretary of the African Association, "had found the Venus enclosed in a cage on a platform raised about three feet above the floor, and that 'on being ordered by her keeper, she came out, and that her appearance was highly offensive to delicacy. . . . The Hottentot was produced like a wild beast, and ordered to move backwards and forwards and come out and go into her cage, more like a bear than a human being.'"[5] However well the horrible conditions seem to meet Demleitner's criteria for evoking empathic responses from the public, Baartman was brought into court to determine her complicity as well as her consent. Parks dramatizes the interrogation of Baartman, when the court seeks to determine if the show was "done with full consent of the fair Hottentot."[6]

In these scenes, eyewitnesses provide "evidence" about their experience as immediate spectator-participants or witnesses to the effects of the experience on others. Piecing together this courtroom scene from various archives and cultural productions, including ballads, captions found in satirical drawings, court documents, and newspaper reporting,

Parks shows that the environment of spectacle extends beyond the exhibit hall. The public space of the courtroom is another circus platform where desire and displacement of accountability supersede the search for clear, balanced truths or the pursuit of justice. The absurdity of the courtroom scenes allows the play's audience to witness the dynamic between Baartman and her spectators and observe the way the spectators project their desires onto her. She cannot be a victim as long as they desire her . . . and want to look at her. Determining whether she has been held against her will becomes a secondary concern to the issue of her display and the effects it has on its audience.

In the courtroom, a widow provides secondhand testimony about her late husband's response to the show. The hyperbolic description of the show invokes two well-known visual representations of the Hottentot exhibit in France, including *Les curieux en extase ou les cordons de souliers,* in which the British public pokes at Baartman's buttocks and peers beneath her costume. The widow reports a deeply ambivalent reaction from her late husband, who undercuts his own compassionate utterances—"Poor Creature," "This is a sight that makes me melancholy!"—by following with the uncontrolled exclamation, "Good God what butts!" The widow surmises, "Thuh shock of her killed him, I think,"[7] a claim that accords tremendous power to Baartman. The spectator testimony reinforces repeatedly the notion that Venus possesses the ability to create chaos. The play forces into focus that the blame shifts to her and her inherent dangerousness. Failure to recognize one's role within the human-rights violation in this case falls on the spectator, the audience that creates the demand and sets the stage for exploitation. The same public that refuses to recognize its own appetites for the dehumanization of others is left in the position to judge whether Baartman can redeem herself.

In the courtroom scenes in the play—as in *Les curieux en extase ou les cordons de souliers*—Venus appears self-contained; although she is clearly exposed in body, there is little sense of her inner experience. What takes center stage, so to speak, are the spectators. Even as witnesses testify that her surroundings always "smelled of shit," they continued to participate. While describing their own repeated consumption/participation in the spectacle, the witnesses, as well as the court officials, accuse Venus of bearing a mark and being inherently filthy. The audience of the play itself is not exempt from this critique. During the play's intermission, the Baron Docteur reads from Venus's autopsy notes while encouraging the audience to take their break. Greg Miller describes the shifting roles: "Here Parks effectively stages *us*; the play presents the 'history' within which we are profoundly uncomfortable, and the intermission stages the audience as wanting something else."[8]

Although Parks makes it clear that the public's desire is on trial here, the play also flirts with the idea that Baartman remains unashamed. "There is no moment, in fact," according to Harry Elam, Jr., and Alice Rayner, "when Saartjie [Sara] really does seem to accept her circumstances or her treatment as shameful. Terrible, filthy, miserable, brutal, but never shameful."[9] Aja Marneweck concurs and adds that "Venus's sexual confidence in the play revolves around her egotistical awareness of the power of her 'deviant' body to titillate and repulse."[10] When "into Court they took her," they do so "To Thus determine if she liked for everyone to look at her."[11] Even in the court's vaudevillian flavor, its line of inquiry invokes serious concerns about the efficacy of survivor testimony within a hostile courtroom and culture. When the court reports that Baartman "says she thinks there is no great harm in showing her backside,"[12] this provocative admission forces a shift in judgment about her role as passive victim.

When the courtroom inquiry changes to condemnation with the court's statement, "Her kind bears Gods bad mark and, baptised or not, they blacken-up the honor of our fair country. Get her out of here!"[13] Venus shifts quickly into the self-deprecating mode required for her survival. Parks suggests the limits of the courtroom when dealing with desire; Venus is only heard when she speaks in the language that moves accountability away from the spectators. It is not until she humbles herself sufficiently that they begin to listen to her voice. Venus makes her case: "Please. Good good honest people. If I bear thuh bad mark what better way to cleanse it off? Showing my sinful person as a caution to you all could, in the Lords eyes, be a sort of repentance and I could wash off my dark mark. I came here black. Give me a chance to leave here white."[14] Using their logic to plead her case, Venus does not appear to be a victim here. She wants to stay. The argument could be made that she has internalized their image of her as a lower being. However, it seems that she makes this statement in direct connection to their statement of concern that she will pollute the public imagination. She relies on the current investment in salvation, manipulating this justification for continuing to pursue a colonialist agenda. When she claims, "To hide yr shame is evil. I show mine. Would you like to see?"[15] she presents the mix of lust and evangelizing that was pervading the public imagination.

Critical response to the play has focused on the questions it raises regarding Baartman's response to her "public." Elam and Rayner describe the play's ambivalence: "On the one hand, Parks's stage presentation re-cuperates and refigures her body as a sign of opposition to colonial exploi-tation and dehumanization. On the other hand, the play represents and reinscribes these same systems of oppression and degradation by putting her once again on display before the gaze of an audience."[16] Where some scholars have read ambivalence in Parks's retelling of the Baartman tale, Jean Young's "The Re-ojectification and Re-commodification of Saartjie Baartman in Suzan-Lori Parks's *Venus*" argues that "Parks's Venus reifies the perverse imperialist mind set, and her mythic historical re-construction subverts the voice of Saartjie Baartman." In her critique, Young privileges her research on the historical records to make claims against Parks's play: "My historicized reading furthers the discourse that considers the issues of power, choice, and agency."[17] Describing her methodology as "a close examination of the circumstances connected with Baartman's removal from the Cape and subsequent exhibition," Young claims that "Baartman was a victim, not an accomplice, not a mutual participant in this demeaning objectification, and Parks's stage representation of her complicity diminishes the tragedy of her life as a nineteenth-century Black woman stripped of her humanity at the hands of a hostile, racist society that held her and those like her in contempt."[18] Relying heavily on eyewitness descriptions found in Richard Altrick's *The Shows of London*, Young seeks to demonstrate that Baartman's treat-ment, severe and demoralizing as the testimony attests, proves that the play's representation exploits rather than redeems.

However, one could argue that the play's ambivalence is the ambiv-alence of the traumatic experience that unsettles humans to the core. Moments of identification with all that violates must be understood within the context of survival. Does the issue of complicity always nec-essarily "diminish" the tragedy? Is it possible that Baartman was not "stripped of her humanity" but that her humanity remains intact within the play?

Many of Young's claims regarding the "re-objectification" in the play seem to respond to Monte Williams's interview with Parks in the *New York Times*, in which Parks claims, "I could have written a two-hour saga with Venus being the victim. But she's multi-faceted. She's vain, beauti-ful, intelligent and yes, complicit. I write about the world of my experi-ence, and it's more complicated than 'that white man down the street is giving me a hard time.' That's just one aspect of our reality. As black people, we're encouraged to be narrow and simply address the race issue. We deserve so much more."[19] Parks expresses the desire to move beyond a static representation of Venus as "poster child" for colonial oppression. This tension between Young and Parks here, along with the issues of representation described earlier, demonstrates the challenges of dealing with the reception of another's traumatic experience.

Baartman's voice was never recorded within her lifetime, except the court record's brief reference to her claim that she consented to exhibiting her body. Critical attention to her story suggests a desire to know her "true" story. The confusion lies, again, in whether she did and could consent. Why does that question intrigue so? Perhaps it intrigues because the truth lies in between, raising questions about the role of art in relation to testimony. As Dominick LaCapra puts it, "Truth claims are neither the only nor always the most important consideration in art and analysis. Of obvious importance are poetic, rhetorical, and performative dimensions of art which not only mark but also make differences historically. . . . Truth claims are nonetheless relevant to works of art both on the level of their general structures or procedures."[20] This reading relies on the experience of others and their perceptions. Again, traumatic experience, such as the one depicted within the courtroom scene, is always already alien and at a remove, even from the victim herself. To approximate an understanding we always represent; there is no way to reconstruct Baartman's experience completely, and since we now understand that trauma cannot be known fully in the moment, but only belatedly as a legacy or an aftermath, we can see both Parks and Young expressing distinct points on the continuum of reactions. Each reaction mixes with the desire of the witness.

For LaCapra, "Being responsive to the traumatic experience of others, notably of victims, implies not the appropriation of their experience, but what I would call empathic unsettlement, which should have stylistic effects or, more broadly, effects in writing which cannot be reduced to formulas or rules of method."[21] Yet as Demleitner discusses, "empathic unsettlement" occurs within when the spectacle of the victim's body satisfies the expectation of its audience. Whether or not the play achieves "empathic unsettlement," it does bring into focus these questions and forces us to explore our needs from victims. What about this story unsettles and explores our response to victims?

Young's essay and other responses to *Venus* reveal our desire to find the markers of victimhood within the representation of Baartman, whose situation resembles in many ways the current plight of trafficked women. The play does indeed tend to downplay the terrible treatment—or at least fails to dwell at any moment on the conditions that would plead her case as a "pure" victim. However, there is something revealed about our own needs here and about the way these needs limit the possibilities for our responses to survivors even as we desire to understand them.

In the courtroom, the allusion to habeas corpus, calling forth the body to the scene, counters the myth-building around Venus, which removes the body from experience and locates it within the context of spectacle. As Harvey Young puts it in his "Touching History: Suzan-Lori Parks, Robbie McCauley, and the Black Body," "The black body, the accumulated and repeated similarities of the embodied experience of black bodies, is a body that is made to be given to be seen. It is a body that is always on display, always on stage, and always in the process of its own exhibition."[22] The play begins by demythologizing Baartman from histories that would reify her status as either savage slut or passive victim.

Parks challenges the "good victim" model that ignores the moments of possible agency—and momentary complicity—that allow the subject to survive and continue to desire more from her circumstances. The scene in which Venus decides her fate and chooses to leave South Africa for the promised land of Europe bares striking resemblance to the discourse of deception and coercion around contemporary human-trafficking discussions, the stock narrative of a girl from an economically exploited area becoming its latest export. In Venus's case, there is the allure of celebrity: "A big town. A boat ride away. Where the streets are paved with gold."[23] This scene plays on the mythical imaginings and culturally familiar scripts.

Baartman's mistreatment is clear from early in the play. What is at question is her response to this treatment. Upon her arrival in England, the Chorus witnesses Venus's experience: "We could stand here and tell her some lies or the bald truth: That her lifell go from rough to worse. . . . Shes sunk. Theres no escape from this place."[24] The evidence of her suffering within the play comes at moments that pass so quickly that there is no time to react, which does not suggest that the play minimizes the suffering; rather, it reveals the way in which daily suffering seems normal if it pervades one's environment. She is kicked and exists in a "filthy cage."[25] The Mother Showman tells the spectators, "Paw her folks. Hands on. Go on have yr pleasure. Her heathen shame is real."[26] The entire environment shames, and *Venus* stages a constant negotiation of our perception of victims and perpetrators.

When Venus contributes ideas about her act, she complicates her position as passive victim. She tells the Mother Showman, "We should spruce up our act. I could speak for them. Say a little poem or something."[27] This expression of agency unsettles; however, when considered in relation to more current understanding about the relationship between the trauma survivor, her environment, and the perpetrator, it becomes less impossible to accept. As trauma expert Judith Herman puts it, "In situations of captivity, the perpetrator becomes the most powerful person in the life of the victim, and the psychology of the victim is shaped by the actions and beliefs of the perpetrator."[28] We know from earlier moments in the play that she has been raped, caged, and forced to witness the revulsion of others as they watched her body. However, as Herman attests, the victim of exploitation can become divorced or alienated from her own body in the moment in order to survive. She can take on the behaviors of the perpetrators against her own body.

Even as Venus asserts her will within the context by identifying with her perpetrators and against her own body, she is threatened. The mother tells her, "Don't push me, Sweetie. Next doors a smoky pub full of drunken men. I just may invite them in one at a time and let them fuck yr brains out," to which Venus replies, "They do it anyway. . . . They come in drunk when yr sleeping. I wanna go. Please."[29] These few simple lines suggest the repeated abuse or exposure to abuse terrorizing Sara Baartman every day. She makes a simple request—for a lock on her door—and is denied and threatened. One wonders if the men come in when Mother Showman is sleeping, as Sara believes, or if they are allowed in for a fee. Clearly, if he/she wished to protect Sara, the lock would be placed on the door. The psychologist Jennifer Freyd claims in her writings on betrayal trauma, "Detecting betrayal can be too dangerous when the natural changes in behavior it provokes would threaten primary dependent relationships. In order to suppress the natural reaction to betrayal in such cases, information blockages in mental processing occur.[30] In Venus's efforts to negotiate with her perpetrator, she exhibits a kind of denial about the extent of her powerlessness.

This captivity-related denial becomes more insidious in Venus's relationship to the Doctor, modeled on the real-life Dr. Cuvier, who dissected Baartman's genitals, the famous Hottentot apron, after her death. The Doctor enters her life as the rescuer, then continues the abuse but on a much deeper, pervasive level. He seduces her, manipulating her desire to be cared for, to be recognized after the dreadful treatment of the sideshow. The Mother Showman's abuse primes her for this last and deadliest seduction and activates survival strategies that include identifying with the perpetrator.

Nowhere in Baartman's history does it suggest that she fell in love with or became sexually involved with Cuvier. In fact, it is understood that he did not see her "apron" until dissecting after her death in 1815. In *Nature's Body: Gender in the Making of Modern Science*, Londa Schiebinger describes Baartman's desire to maintain her privacy when the scientists tried to persuade her to reveal her apron; in their observations and later dissection, they "relegated her to the world of brute flesh."[31] However, T. Denean Sharpley-Whiting's reading of the Cuvier examination finds it imbued with desire: "Cuvier's gaze, it appears, is tempered with eroticism. . . . Wrenched from the seductive reverie induced by this African Delilah, the scientist violently readjusts his optic receiver and pen."[32] Parks allows insight into the psyche of the perpetrator and the intimacy of the traumatic bond by connecting them intimately within the play. The Baron Doctor represents the ultimate perpetrator, and his relationship with Baartman unsettles most because it involves the deepest betrayal. It reveals the paradoxical intimacy involved in traumatic experience, when one is unmade—macerated, dissected—before another who has complete control.

"To know is to put oneself in danger," according to Jennifer Freyd. "To not know is to align oneself with the caregiver and ensure survival."[33] Venus, instead of recognizing her peril, fantasizes about her power over the Doctor: "He spends all his time with me because he loves me. He hardly visits her at all. She may be his wife all right but shes all dried up. He is not thuh most thrilling lay Ive had but his gold makes up thuh difference and hhh I love him."[34] In this moment, we can also consider what Parks offers to our understanding of resilience. Venus may appear vain or greedy within this moment; however, as contradictory as it may seem, the audience also witnesses a survival strategy at work.

While the Venus attempts to preserve a sense of control and safety by recognizing only the possibility of love, the Chorus voices urge the Doctor to follow his ambition, reminding him, "She'll make uh splendid corpse,"[35] and suggesting the internal struggle within a perpetrator. Ambition colludes with social pressure in the form of the blackmailing Gradeschool Chum, who chides the Doctor, "you reek of Hottentot-amour, Sir, and as a colleague its my duty to speak plain, Sir: we all smell it!"[36] At another moment, the minor character Bride-to-Be sits reading her love letters as the Baron Doctor reads his notes on the dissection, reinforcing again the connection between intimacy and betrayal. Both readings entail a projection of fantasy and fulfillment—a lot like the love letters, a love "fabricated much like this epistle."[37] The Doctor's notes lose the cover of their scientific objectivity when placed alongside the letter-reading woman. We witness the construction of a being through language. She is unmade as he is made, the ultimate gesture of ownership. In this scene and in the later dissection scenes, we gain insight into the psyche of the perpetrator. He has indeed betrayed Venus and exploited her—despite his high standing within the scientific community and gestures toward finding some higher scientific truth. In the end, a perpetrator is one who is able to objectify the body of another to fulfill some appetite. In the midst of these appetites, discussions about choice become irrelevant.

Through the dissection, we see what it means to traumatize, to unmake the world of another. Elaine Scarry claims, "Physical pain is able to obliterate psychological pain because it obliterates all psychological content, painful, pleasurable, and neutral." Pain bestows on the perpetrator the "power to end all aspects of self and world."[38] In an analysis of medicalized killing that allowed Nazi doctors to remain detached and rationalize the killing of millions of people, Robert Jay Lifton describes a reasoning that involved remaining faithful to their Hippocratic oaths. They rationalized the killing as part of a plan that preserved humanity as a whole by identifying and eliminating a "diseased" part.[39] In colonialist discourse, Anne Fausto-Sterling posits that "identifying foreign lands as female helped to naturalize their rape and exploitation."[40] Parks's play underscores the perversity of this identification process, which allows the minor character the Young Man to describe what seems like contemporary sex tours—"Uncle took Dad to Africa. Showed Dad stuff. Blew Dads mind"[41]—and the Doctor to have sexual relations with a woman he plans to dissect posthumously.

In a paradoxical strategy for survival, Venus internalizes this perversity. The play's gloss about chocolate invokes its association with women and psychic distress, noting, "Chocolate is a recognized emotional stimulant, for doctors have recently noticed the tendency of some persons, especially women, to go on chocolate binges either after emotionally upsetting incidents or in an effort to handle an incident which may be emotionally upsetting."[42] Signaling the relationship between chocolate and stress changes the reading of Baartman's relationship to chocolate and alcohol as substances that allow her to manage her anxiety. Consuming chocolates conspicuously, Venus both expresses her own anxious desire and enacts her identification with her perpetrators. She recognizes images that suggest the contours of her own body and then consumes herself in that moment; a sense of doubleness occurs in that moment, indicating her identification with herself as consumable object.

In traumatic alienation, she removes herself from her own bodily experience and consumes the effigy.

"Simple compliance," Judith Herman offers, "rarely satisfies" a perpetrator in relation to his captive. Instead, Herman continues, "he appears to have a psychological need to justify his crimes, and for this he needs the victim's affirmation. Thus he relentlessly demands from his victim professions of respect, gratitude, or even love. His ultimate goal appears to be the creation of a willing victim."[43]

By introducing the love dynamic, *Venus* addresses what remains unspoken within other historical or cultural records. It uses an event that cannot be proven to speak for all such truths. This is what art offers, as LaCapra suggests. In all likelihood there was seduction and love, in no particular order. There were complex interactions that included on some level a degree of consent or desire or willingness to please and be pleased. This is not new territory. What needs checking is our response to these possibilities and our failure then to read that trauma occurs within or because of this intimacy. Perhaps above all else, Suzan-Lori Parks's *Venus* puts these unforgiving and rigid expectations to the test.

Chapters 3 and 4 address the legacy of this traumatic experience as it has been transmitted within the dominant discourse's scripting of the black female body and as it has been lived by survivors. Robbie McCauley's *Sally's Rape* and Gayl Jones's *Corregidora* both examine the exploited ancestral body and the damaged sexual inheritance passed down through distortions of this body's violation within public and familial memory.

3 /   Between Women: Trauma, Witnessing, and the
Legacy of Interracial Rape in Robbie McCauley's
Sally's Rape

At one critical moment in Robbie McCauley's play *Sally's Rape*, the African American McCauley and her white co-performer Jeannie Hutchins engage in a revealing exchange about history, trauma, and denial:

ROBBIE: In 1964 at the library job a U.S. history major who'd graduated from Smith College said—
JEANNIE: I never knew white men did anything with colored women on the plantations.
ROBBIE: I said "It was rape." Her eyes turned red. She choked on her sandwich and quit the job.[1]

Through this exchange and throughout *Sally's Rape*, McCauley asks her audience to explore what it means to "choke" on a repressed history. When asked about the creative motivation behind her Obie-winning play *Sally's Rape*, Robbie McCauley responds, "I did this series out of the obsession for examining my feelings of survival."[2] Centered on the rape of McCauley's great-great-grandmother Sally, a former slave, McCauley's performance bears witness to surviving a traumatized personal and cultural history. Ann E. Nymann refers to *Sally's Rape* as "a social experiment in which Robbie McCauley, an African-American performance artist, performs the black female subject out of victimization."[3] McCauley's "social experiment," particularly as it relates to exploring traumatic legacies that haunt contemporary bodies, represents the work of feminist performance artists who emerged on the experimental theater scene in the late 1980s and early 1990s, such Holly Hughes, Karen

Finley, and Peggy Shaw, and who used the performance genre to explore the female body as a cultural text. Rebecca Schneider, who said that her experience at a 1991 Kitchen performance of *Sally's Rape* felt like "an act of spectating more akin to ritual than entertainment,"[4] addresses the "explicit body" found in these feminist performances: "A mass of orifices and appendages, the explicit body in representation is foremost a site of social markings, physical parts, and gestural signatures of gender, race, class, age, sexuality—all of which bear ghosts of historical meaning."[5] Part of a series that includes *Indian Wars* and *My Father and the Wars,* *Sally's Rape* focuses on the connection between family and the unspeakable within personal and collective memory. McCauley uses family anecdotes and her own experience to begin the process of uncovering the denial of sexual violence against black women and the damage caused by this denial. Indeed, like Rufel's complex response to witnessing the scars on Dessa's genital area in *Dessa Rose,* the Smith graduate's response in the quoted dialogue from the play exemplifies the kind of experience that McCauley calls forth in her work: that is, a bodily reaction to what has remained unspoken within dominant collective memory, in part because knowledge has been transmitted by writers like Nehemiah and scientists such as Cuvier. This connection of body and memory—or refusal of memory—is linked to the complex dynamic found in cross-racial encounters that raise traumatic histories and questions of survival in public space.

The performance has a conversational style between the two performers and the audience members, making it feel intimate and familiar while also evoking the tension of discovery. With its sparse set and the two women in equally simple dresses to offset the complexity of their emotional responses, the performance explores what Douglas Crimp and Thomas Keenan refer to as "socially produced trauma,"[6] or the psychic damage caused by societal indifference to suffering, or failed witness. According to trauma experts such as Judith Herman, Dori Laub, and Bessel van der Kolk, trauma involves a delay in response. The emotional and physical responses not experienced initially are raised when the survivor perceives a potential threat in a new situation, causing the survivor to relive on a physiological level the terror of the original experience. The embodied memory is experienced without a direct link to the "story" of the original experience. In this way, the experience of memory has been fractured. Traumatic memory exists in two distinct forms: the relentlessly recurring image, stereotyped and static, and the unconscious bodily response to conditions that bear psychic resemblance to the original experience. Recovery requires a reintegration of fractured memory forms. This reintegration occurs when the original trauma survivor processes the story with a willing witness who assists the survivor in understanding the connections between the actual event and its impact on her life. However, failing to recognize the survivor's experience, on a cultural as well as individual level, reproduces traumatic experience.

In "The AIDS Crisis Is Not Over," Keenan elaborates on the role that public denial plays in exacerbating the effects of the original trauma: "There's a double trauma here. On the one hand, there's a cataclysmic event, which produces symptoms and calls for testimony. And then it happens again, when the value of the witness in the testimony is denied, and there's no one to hear the account, no one to attend or respond— not simply to the event, but to its witness as well."[7] Although Keenan makes these points within a discussion on the AIDS crisis, his theorizing around the problems of social accountability identifies the devastating effects of the public denial on survivors of other forms of trauma. The "socially produced trauma" enacted in the library scene entails a lack of recognition of the survivor's story that reinforces shame in the survivor and denies the implication of others in the traumatic history.

The two performers in *Sally's Rape* stage what Antonius C. G. M. Robben refers to as a "contestive relation" in cultural memory, "which keeps [opposing cultural groups] hostage to each other's memory politics. . . . People cannot mourn their losses when others deny that those losses took place."[8] Efforts to mourn are undermined by this denial; Robben suggests, "The contest of memory denies conflicting parties sufficient room to work through their traumas, hinders them from gradually standing back from the past and proceeding from testimony to historical interpretation and from re-experience to commemoration."[9] *Sally's Rape* dramatizes this "contestive relation" in cultural memory around interracial rape and its legacy.

The white woman who chokes on her sandwich refuses to claim her connection to the history that McCauley's character describes. In this scene, she is not being asked to accept blame for the rape. Rather, her responsibility lies in acknowledging the history, and in not remaining outside the grasp of this history, untouched and untouchable. Thomas Keenan explains:

> There's a way in which the telling of the story, the testimony of the affected community, functions or can be received as an accusation,

by those who thought they were uninvolved. The testimony is an address, which means it's a provocation to a response. And that's what they don't want to give. They don't want to respond to the person who has called—for responsibility. When someone says "I don't want to hear about it," or counters with a slur, they are telling the truth. They are creating themselves as something insulated in its generality from the specificity of address, by disavowing any involvement with one who appeals.[10]

When McCauley forces the young white woman to face the knowledge of the systematic rape of black women, she disrupts the transmission of traumatic memory that allows whites to forget the painful history of race relations. In *Dessa Rose*, Rufel's response to seeing Dessa's scars changes the white woman's relationship not only to the former slave but also to herself and the culture in which she was raised. However, the white woman in the library scene refuses to recognize the "scars" presented through the exchange and does more than become embarrassed or uncomfortable. She also continues to "create herself" as the epitome of a privileged white womanhood, insulated and protected from the knowledge of our racial history, unwilling to hear its ugly truths. She quits the job, thereby removing herself as a recipient of the address, reproducing what Hilary Harris refers to as "White Woman's 'nature' of purity (in heart, mind, and most problematically, flesh), her 'innocence,' for which she is most known, and, perhaps, most knowable to herself."[11] Through this failed address, the culturally constructed identity described by Harris remains intact.

According to Evelynn Hammonds, "black women's sexuality has been constructed in a binary opposition to that of white women: it is rendered simultaneously invisible, visible (exposed), hypervisible, and pathologized in dominant discourses."[12] In the preceding chapter, this construction was dramatized in Suzan-Lori Parks's *Venus*, particularly in the courtroom spectacle. As Hammonds suggests, the construction of racial difference is dependent on binary opposition in which whiteness embodies all positive cultural value and blackness its opposite. The dynamic between McCauley and Jeannie Hutchins exposes the social construction of a racialized gender identity that allows for both the exploitation of black female bodies and the suppression of that traumatic history of interracial rape within collective memory. Testimony is both found and denied in the way the black woman and the white woman reflect against or read each other's bodies and in their acknowledgment or denial of the ways their bodies are used in dominant culture. The testimony that *Sally's Rape* creates involves what Joseph Roach defines as genealogies of performance that "attend to . . . the reciprocal reflections" that bodies "make on one another's surfaces" during interracial encounters. These encounters, such as the one demonstrated in the library scene, provide insight into what Roach refers to as "the disparities between history as it is discursively transmitted and memory as it is publicly enacted by the bodies that bear its consequences."[13] The library scene demonstrates this "disparity" and stages a vivid moment of transition in the "reciprocal reflections" between black and white women, revealing the ways in which history links the gender and racial identity of these two women inextricably.

The body, memory, and the "reciprocal reflections" function in several ways in *Sally's Rape*. McCauley deals with the traumatized black female body in historical and psychological terms. Frantz Fanon's writings explore the ways in which public encounters between black and white bodies evoke racism's complex history, supporting Roach's "reciprocal reflections" argument and providing an important theoretical basis for understanding McCauley's work. As mentioned in the introduction to this book, in *Black Skin, White Masks* Fanon describes a scene in public space when a terrified child points at him and yells, "Look, a Negro!"[14] The young child's words force Fanon to feel alienated from his own body:

> Then, assailed at various points, the corporeal schema crumbled, its place taken by the racial epidermal schema. In the train it was no longer a question of being aware of my body in the third person but in the triple person. In the train I was given not one but two, three places. . . . It was not that I was finding febrile coordinates in the world. I existed triple: I occupied space. I moved toward the other . . . and the evanescent other, hostile but not opaque, transparent, not there, disappeared.
>
>   Nausea. . . . [15]

In this encounter, history, both as it was lived by ancestral bodies and as Fanon has inherited it through colonial discourse, bears its full, violent weight on him. Confronted with his body's representation within a history that denies his humanity, Fanon's finds his own bodily experience altered. This alienation results when his very senses must compete with the "thousand details, anecdotes, stories" that make claims about his historical inferiority in relation to whiteness.[16]

This contrast between the "historico-racial schema," the cultural narratives that reproduce racial hegemony, and the lived experience of that body suggests Foucault's description of genealogy, which "as an analysis of descent, is thus situated within the articulation of the body and history."[17] The "task" of genealogy, according to Foucault, "is to expose a body totally imprinted by history and the process of history's destruction of the body."[18] Fanon's response to this disorienting assault reveals the urgent need to reclaim his body from this psychic destruction: "I thought what I had in hand was to construct a physiological self, to balance space, to localize sensations."[19] His desire to "balance space, to localize sensation," stems from the dislocation happening within that moment. His encounter with the child reveals the way history is enacted through what Roach refers to as the "reciprocal reflections they make on one another's surfaces as they foreground their capacities for interaction."[20] In the encounter, whiteness is represented by a child, signifying the way whiteness is constituted by a kind of innocence in the face of history's terror. The scene reflects the ability of whiteness to remain new, untainted and free from history's consequences, by always projecting the horror away from itself, like the child pointing at Fanon's body or the Smith graduate in the library scene.

The analysis of the body done by Roach, Foucault, and Fanon proves useful when examining Robbie McCauley's attempt in *Sally's Rape* to confront the "historico-racial schema" or genealogy of the black female body within the dominant white culture. McCauley's attempts to "balance space, localize sensation" represent a desire to find a means to articulate her own experience and the bodily response to the traumatic history she has inherited. The *Sally's Rape* performance exposes the construction of these bodies, bringing psychic processes into public space. It becomes important to examine how culture traumatizes memory, leaving memory in the body to be reenacted in each encounter while denying survivors an opportunity to express the phenomenon. Theater in this case reproduces the social space in which original traumas occurred, making the encounter visible for the audience.

Returning to the body as a site of information related to pain, McCauley must work through the way bodies have been constructed racially and sexually in the public sphere. She distinguishes the "historico-racial" body from the experience of pain associated with traumatic history, while also making it clear that the reproduction of the "historical-racial" scheme perpetuates the failure of testimony. If the distinction between these two bodies is not addressed, then McCauley risks that the audience will not recognize the suffering she tries to convey. However, the performance strives for accountability that moves beyond a sense of cathartic release during the performance. Jill Dolan describes the strategy employed by performance artists such as McCauley, who do not allow audience members to settle into well-worn responses in reaction to controversial material. In *The Feminist Spectator as Critic*, Dolan posits that in performance such as McCauley's, "the representational apparatus is ideologically marked, its material aspects must be brought into full view and denaturalized for the spectator's inspection. The mystification of social arrangements is exposed and the spectator is presented with the possibility of change.[21] *Sally's Rape* marks the "representational apparatus"— the stage directions, set, costumes, and dialogue—repeatedly during the performance by bringing the audience into the process. Hutchins cues them with lines such as, "Let's practice with something from the context of the piece."[22] In this way, the performance is more complicated than the telling of a painful story and the release of powerful emotions. As McCauley tells Vivian Patraka, "It's fine if it's an exorcism for an audience member, but I see it more as an opening for movement, as creating a groundwork for dialogue. The idea of releasing for its own sake means that you then don't move anywhere. I prefer when people say, 'You made me think; I disagreed with you, but I was moved to think.'"[23] Thinking in this case means developing an awareness of the interactions between a live audience and a performer, which also entails an awareness of what it means to view a black, female body in public space fraught with an unspoken racist history.

In *Sally's Rape*, McCauley uses the theater to create a new public space for the construction of the address to articulate the traumatic history and the complex cultural processes that keep this history muted. The public, interactive nature of live performance allows for the exploration of the process of bearing witness to traumatic histories. Both performers walk freely around the stage and engage the audience members often, blurring the creative boundaries between performers and audience. Playwright and educator Karen Malpede clarifies the efficacy of relating current theories on post-traumatic response, particularly in relation to the intersubjective dynamic of witnessing that has been identified as essential to the survivor's process of making meaning: "Because theatre takes place in public and involves the movement of bodies across a stage, theatre seems uniquely suited to portray the complex interpersonal realities of trauma and to give shape to the compelling interventions that become possible when trauma is addressed by others who validate the victim's reality."[24] Malpede has developed the idea of the "witnessing imagination," a strategy in theater through which "the witness, whether journalist or therapist, playwright, actor, or audience, offers his/her body to the one who testifies in order quite literally to help bear the tale. The witnessing experience is visceral—information resonates inside the bodies of both the teller and the receivers of testimony, and in this process both are changed."[25] According to Malpede, whose ideas about witnessing have been influenced by Dori Laub and Shoshana Felman's collaborative efforts,[26] witnessing is an exchange or encounter that occurs at a bodily level.

The performance between McCauley, Hutchins, and the audience invokes what Dori Laub refers to as the "third level of witnessing,"[27] in which the process of bearing witness to traumatic experience is analyzed and understood. The performance itself bears witness not only to the facts of interracial rape but also to the dynamic of denial that reproduces the traumatizing effect of the initial violence by silencing and isolating the survivor. If the response is that audience members do not wish to claim their part, which mostly entails owning a responsibility for understanding the history and its implications in daily life, then the performance forces this denial and evasion into the public space. Through the exchange between McCauley and Hutchins, the performance constructs another address, one involving McCauley, Jeannie Hutchins, and the audience. "I want to engage in dialogue about subject matter that there are emotional barriers to," McCauley says. "In what we do, the audience becomes a character."[28]

McCauley, Hutchins, and the audience-as-character form a witnessing relation that counters the failed address and socially produced trauma exemplified by the Smith graduate in the library scene. If, as Hilary Harris suggests, "racist whiteness is understood as constructed through the shifting historical relations between peoples of color and whites, as well as within 'the internal hierarchies of whiteness,' then it is crucial to develop understandings of antiracist whiteness," which, Harris claims, "must perform new relations with the subjectivities, the ideologies, and the material legacies of those historical relations."[29] McCauley, Hutchins, and the audience do "perform new relations" in *Sally's Rape* by making visible the "old" relations, the "contestive relations" that include the failed address evidenced within the library scene. Immediately following Hutchins's portrayal of the Smith graduate, she distances herself from the character and begins a critical dialogue with McCauley and the audience to look more closely at that moment of failed address. When Hutchins asks the audience, "Was the Smith College graduate denying . . . ? lying . . . ? or dumb . . . ? Yeah she was dumb. I keep telling you that,"[30] she encourages the audience to make the connection between socially produced trauma and a kind of public forgetting linked to racial privilege. This connection continues to resonate throughout the performance.

In a moment of dialogue with Hutchins, McCauley explains her feelings about the selective amnesia that seems to define whiteness: "It angers me that even though your ancestors might have been slaves—because they did have white slaves . . . only made black slavery mandatory for economic reasons, so they could catch us when we ran away—that history has given you the ability to forget your shame about being oppressed by being ignorant, mean, or idealistic . . . which makes it dangerous for me."[31]

The "invisibility" of whiteness that led to the marking of black bodies for slavery has also, as McCauley exposes, allowed whites to escape the mark of history. The performance suggests that the collective amnesia around traumatic histories of racialized others is part of the reproduction of white privilege. The performance reveals that the dominant racial order sustains itself by using the broken memory of traumatized others and the denial accompanying perpetration to encourage forgetting on a cultural level. McCauley refers to "these new ones with the alligators," who "act like they wadn't born with no memory."[32] The "alligators" suggest the label of a clothing brand worn by a certain cultural type: young, white, and affluent. Invisibility of whiteness coincides with the erasure of memory. To be born with no memory is to admit no responsibility toward the past, to deny history's claim on one's body. When referring to the dangerous implications of this amnesia, McCauley acknowledges that the forgetting occurs at her expense. Without understanding history, the discrepancies between black and white material reality are used to justify theories of white supremacy. Coming to terms with traumatic histories involves sorting through the painful fragments of memory and understanding their relationship to privilege and the bodies bearing their legacy.

McCauley is direct about the antiracist commitment within her work. Specifically, she defines the racism her work addresses as "White supremacy" or "The idea that white people are something special and that to identify with the white condition is a good thing that has been so much a part of European colonial thinking that so-called white people and colonized people all over the world have internalized the thought for centuries."[33] Confronting this "internalized" thought presents its challenges, McCauley acknowledges: "People easily bristle at these state-ments. People who consider themselves white may be tired of being put in the role of the oppressor, and may feel there's nothing they can do about it."[34] In a compelling analysis of interracial dialogue in McCauley's work, Deborah Thompson describes the paucity of "productive interra-cial configurations" and identifies the "critical problems" as "how both to acknowledge (even insist on acknowledging) and to disavow histori-cal paradigms of interracial relations, and how to create more produc-tive paradigms without acting as if we're performing on a clean stage."[35] Indeed, the performance attempts to look at socially produced trauma without reproducing a failed address through accusation, denial, or evasion. McCauley explains her desire to create a space in which col-lective remembering can happen: "I am being a witness by choosing to remember. What's important about witnessing is that the audience is doing it with me. One of the problems with modern industrial society is the disconnection from that constant witnessing of the past, of where we came from, of being with the stories, and so that's my work."[36] Her work involves creating a connection with the audience, to avoid alienat-ing them and to encourage an open environment where the tough issues can be aired in public. While McCauley introduces issues of survival, she shares resources and creates a community.

During the performance, the audience is offered food as a gesture of community. But the introduction of food here is more than just a welcom-ing gesture on McCauley's part. It becomes difficult to forget one's body while eating. The food functions as a reminder of material reality and of the consumption of the past in the present, grounding the abstractions of history in the bodily engagement with memory. Comparing the body as lived to the body in representation is crucial to McCauley's project, as the scene with the Smith graduate "choking on" history attests, and the food strategy initiates the audience into a communal, participatory space that moves beyond that moment in the library.

As McCauley passes out food, she informs audience members that they will assist in the creation of a dialogue, and she allays possible tension by providing reassuring and explicit directions. "We'll use hand signals," she tells them, "lead like camp directors, divide you into groups. . . . Well, it doesn't matter what section you're in, just matters who you are, and you can change your opinion as time goes on."[37] Through this method, McCauley hopes to create a space for connection between the audience and the material of the performance: "Well, in this work I continually explain what I'm doing as part of the form. And I'm not trying to push people away. It's the ritual aspect, the joining that's important. Even though I often exaggerate difference, I make it possible to explore what I'm doing with the audience's participation."[38] She addresses the audience so that they can move beyond an accuser/accused dichotomy while continuing to focus on the implications of a racist history. She guides the audience through a variety of responses toward the fear involved in facing the truth: fear of being accused or exposed as ignorant or inherently evil.

At a crucial moment in the performance, McCauley stands naked on an auction block as Hutchins coaches the audience into bidding for her. "I wanted to do this," she tells them afterward, "stand naked in public on the auction block. I thought somehow it could help free us from this. (*Refers to her naked body*) Any old socialist knows, one can't be free till all are free."[39] McCauley's body elicits a response that reconnects audience members with a sense of their own body in history. Her vulnerability to the pain of that history becomes contagious and allows her audience to transcend their roles as passive observers, involving and implicating their own unspoken relationship to the horrors of the past, particularly in relation to the spectacle of the suffering McCauley embodies.

During the auction-block moment, McCauley travels to the site of a specific historical trauma, the point at which white supremacy enacted its claim to the black female body in public space. She returns to reclaim what was lost in this moment, what Bibi Bakare-Yusuf refers to as "the possession of a voice" in public space. According to Bakare-Yusuf,

> The possession of voice becomes significant for both torturer and tortured. For the torturer, the awareness of voice confirms his power, his existence, the presence of a world; for the sufferer, the absence of a world, the awareness of his/her corporeality, the limits of his/her extension in the world. This has been precisely the claim of feminist and black theorists, who have pointed out that the association of blacks and females with corporeality excludes and debars them from the public sphere that makes subjectivity possible.[40]

In the transformation from silent object to the speaking subject, McCauley confronts the history of her body as possession. She must deal with the issue of possession from within as well, as she confronts the overwhelming effects of trauma on the body.

Telling the story, creating a narrative from the seemingly unspeakable, undermines the process of silencing bodies. McCauley's performance reveals how memory has been buried in the body, outside language and without a sense of space in cultural imagination. This burying of memory is linked to the isolating effects of trauma that erase collective subjectivity and alienate the survivor from herself and her surroundings. The performance acknowledges that the audience members must be made conscious of their perceptions of the naked body, or of how they are implicated in the historical-racial scheme described by Fanon, to understand their participation in racism's own form of traumatic repetition. To stage their interactions and dialogues around issues such as sexuality and the construction of femininity is to allow insight into the way these constructions have worked within history and how they have exposed the black female body to sexual trauma.

Nellie McKay refers to rape as "the most direct common threat" faced by all women, and she continues by asking, "How then do we account for the fact that the most irreconcilable angers, jealousies, and hostilities plaguing relationships between women of color and white women have their genesis in the politics of sexuality and, to a large extent, in those of rape?"[41] The dissonance to which McKay refers played itself out most visibly during the second wave of feminism in the United States, when women writers of color, most notably Angela Davis, criticized the antirape movement for scapegoating African American men. In *Against Our Will*, white feminist Susan Brownmiller refers to interracial rape as "a national obsession."[42] Brownmiller's chapter on interracial rape criticizes antilynching activist Ida B. Wells for discrediting white women. Wells, according to Brownmiller, "subordinates sexual to racial"[43] and, in doing so, conforms to the misogyny within the larger culture despite her radical intentions.

Angela Davis argues that Brownmiller and other white writers in the antirape movement subordinate racial to sexual: "If Black women have been conspicuously absent from the ranks of the contemporary anti-rape movement, it may be due, in part, to that movement's indifferent posture toward the frame-up rape charge as an incitement to racist aggression."[44] According to Davis, white feminists such as Brownmiller invoke stereotypes about African American sexuality, both male and female, and "historical myopia further prevents them from comprehending that the portrayal of Black men as rapists reinforces racism's open invitation to white men to avail themselves sexually of Black women's bodies."[45] Davis argues that the stereotypes work together within a collective unconscious shaped by the racist ideology that marks black sexuality as wild, dangerous, and animalistic. In contrast, white womanhood, at least publicly, is associated with the institutions of motherhood and marriage and must be protected from sexual predation.

Sally's Rape participates in this controversial dialogue around interracial rape. Valerie Smith suggests that "interracial rape operates as a site where ideologies of racial and gender differences come into tension with and interrogate each other."[46] *Sally's Rape* focuses on this site and examines the point at which cultural constructions of identity connect with trauma to make and unmake subjectivity along racial, sexual, and class lines. Within the aesthetic space of performance, the connections between identity, history, and subject positions are uncovered as a process, one that is linked to the perception of gendered/racialized identity in public space. In "Feminism as a Persistent Critique of History," bell hooks remarks, "Given the way in which sexism continues to shape the way women thinkers are seen, the moment women disagree, conflict is reduced to pure spectacle."[47] McCauley and Hutchins attempt to move beyond the spectacle by first acknowledging and confronting it directly. They engage in a dialogue on the representation of racialized bodies and the way this representation has contributed historically to socially produced trauma caused by the failure to validate the place of the witness and the survivor.

McCauley expresses frustration about trying to create a performance when the vehicle of transmission—language—remains saturated with an ideology hostile to her testimony. Hutchins worries that she will be unmasked by playing these roles, exposed as naive, indifferent, and self-absorbed in her whiteness:

ROBBIE: What upsets me is language. I can't win in your language.
JEANNIE: You're going to win anyway. What upsets me is there's an underlying implication that you're gonna get underneath something and pull it out. That you can see it and I can't.[48]

In the play, McCauley and Hutchins sit across from each other during a dialogue about the limits of language. As they speak, they hold each other's hands and push back and forth between right and left sides in a continuous rocking motion. There is a sense that their bodies are laboring under the words, struggling to commit but in need of the repetitive motion to quiet any defensiveness that may seek to protect them from each other.

To return to Sherley Anne Williams's observations, "As the object of an almost always illicit desire and the butt of ribald, taunting jokes, the white woman is one of the most traditional figures in the culture and history of Black people in America."[49] Jeannie Hutchins voices concern about the possibility of being objectified and mocked within the performance. "One of the good jokes about *Sally's Rape*," McCauley explains, "is that Jeannie Hutchins and I had a long talk about whether or not she was playing 'the stupid white girl.' And it's not that, it's the two of us enjoying the dialogue about my stuff."[50] Hutchins's concern that she will be the "stupid white girl" is countered by McCauley's insistence on the significance of listening to each other's words throughout the performance.[51]

For McCauley these experiences with audiences have provided a deepening sense of the work's purpose, which, she explains, is about talking and listening. Understanding and developing the relationship between teller and listener, or between witnesses, around issues of trauma and memory surfaces as an important goal within the work. McCauley tells her family story to the audience, but Hutchins is the first witness, the one who heard the story behind the scenes and then becomes part of the process of telling it. Immediately after the library scene, Hutchins disidentifies with the white woman who denies the interracial rape of black women and the sexual violence of slavery. Hutchins's participation invokes the history of the relation between white women, race, and rape, and yet McCauley and Hutchins make a conscious effort to decenter the white woman's body. When McCauley reminds Hutchins that the performance is not about her but that it is McCauley's story that Hutchins performs with her, she makes clear that whiteness will not be allowed to claim "center stage," even if it is in an attempt to understand white racism. The performance opens with a prologue, "Talking about What It Is About." In this opening, Hutchins tells McCauley, "Well, that one person said it was about you and me. And I know it's not about me, but it's about you and I'm in it." McCauley responds, "It's my story, and you're in it because I put you in it."[52]

The performance takes a stand against the reproduction of narratives that convey personal experience without affirming a sense of commitment and responsibility to an ongoing dialogue. In this way, *Sally's Rape* contests the usefulness of consciousness-raising formats, which according to Kimberly Christensen have their limits in a multicultural feminist movement: "The CR [conscious-raising] mode of knowledge production, while appropriate and accurate for people seeking to understand and challenge their own oppression, often simply replicates rationalizations for inequality when used by oppressors to understand their own experience."[53] The performance does not allow Hutchins to remember her experience with racial difference as apolitical or innocent. Instead, she is constantly reminded of her privileged position and its direct relation to African American history. She cannot tell a story that allows her to understand her experience outside this context.

For example, when Hutchins wants to claim her desire to be Billie Holiday, she is immediately reminded that her understanding of what it means to be Billie Holiday comes from the idealization of suffering and the erasure of her connection as a white woman to Holiday's specific history. Her desire to be Billie Holiday seems naive and reveals more about the way white mainstream culture can make pain romantic and appealing. If she had expressed her desire to be Billie Holiday outside the performance, she may have been met with a more receptive response, with the tragedy of Holiday's life seeming beautiful and somehow glamorous. But when read within the historical context and the lingering presence of raw pain evoked by the performance, the idealism about Holiday seems self-centered and naive. It reveals more about Hutchins's desire and the consumption of black female suffering. McCauley also tells the story of an uncle who was forced to eat "the whole bucket of fatback and greens" in front of a white audience, "until he commenced to rolling on the floor and passing gas, and they laughed and laughed . . . and the ladies too."[54] The story about the uncle and the allusion to Billie Holiday each suggests white culture's propensity toward fetishizing black suffering. However, like the courtroom scene and intermission in Parks's *Venus*, *Sally's Rape* explores the perception of black suffering in public space, shifting the focus from the spectacle of the body and toward the white spectator's role in the creation of the scene.

It is important to examine Hutchins's role within the context of a growing movement of racial consciousness involving whiteness. In *White Women, Race Matters: The Social Construction of Whiteness*, Ruth Frankenberg writes that "white women's senses of self, other, identity, and worldview are also racialized, for they emerged here as repositories of the key elements of the history of the idea of race, in the United States and beyond."[55] In McCauley's work as a teacher and director, she recommends that individuals reconstruct this inventory and "encourage[s] white actors to take the material of how their families participated in, or received privileges from, the horrors of racism and take time to think about it."[56] This critical self-reflection is necessary for the kind of dialogue and social change that McCauley's performance promotes.

The "reciprocal reflections" between McCauley and Hutchins often involve exposing the class distinctions used to define white and black femininity. Connections between material conditions, exposure to trauma, and issues of survival resonate powerfully in *Sally's Rape*. References to class mark the distinction between the consumption of material resources and the labor of female bodies according to race. The Smith graduate represents a privileged position, and the moment when she chokes on her sandwich marks a break in her conspicuous consumption of the resources she has inherited at the expense of others. McCauley and Hutchins invoke socialism to discuss white women's relationship to the material resources gained through their position:

JEANNIE: Rosa Luxemburg had no patience for bourgeois women who
    didn't work. She called them—
ROBBIE: Co-consumptive
JEANNIE: More parasitic than parasites.[57]

The white woman in the library seems to demonstrate a parasitic relationship to the past as her ignorance of history allows her to maintain her status. Although she works, the Smith woman also has the ability to quit the job and remove herself from the space, refusing the testimony she has received within it. The encounter takes places within a library, the repository of information, a public place in which particular kinds of knowledge have been archived. In this public space, the black woman labors while the white woman consumes, or rejects, knowledge. When the black woman voices an alternative to the dominant historical narrative, one that contradicts the version taught at Smith College and archived within the library, she challenges the white woman's consumption of knowledge and resources.

In another scene, McCauley and Hutchins discuss comportment and "lady-like behavior." As McCauley tells Vivian Patraka, "So much of it has to do with sexuality. Black women particularly struggle to deal with the image of the saint and the whore, or the church lady and the slut."[58] Black women's struggle to define themselves against the stereotypes of promiscuity resulted in close attention to "proper" behavior. The scene undoes the association between white women and a kind of naturally pure femininity that needs to be saved from corrupting influences. McCauley has to correct Hutchins on the placement of her legs. The scene also demonstrates McCauley's struggle with the internalization of shame. She needs to adhere to rigid protocol in an attempt to avoid danger. The white woman appears to enjoy a greater sense of security, protection, and safety in the world due in part to her perceived fragility.

This safety is an illusion, of course, because white women must deal with the threat of rape as well, but *Sally's Rape* forces into focus the ways in which race and class affect the experience of this threat.

The critical difference between the two women in relation to the legacy of trauma and public space is most evident at two specific moments within the performance, which also mark the limits of the testimonial encounter between witness and listener. The first critical moment occurs when Hutchins refuses to stand naked on the auction block. In this refusal, she acknowledges the limitations of cross-racial solidarity and her position of privilege in social and emotional terms. Hutchins does not have a connection to the violated body on the auction block. McCauley, however, cannot avoid the inheritance that the public nakedness represents. The two women do not share the history, and this profound difference influences their experience of their bodies in the present as well. Instead of smoothing over these differences, *Sally's Rape* forces them to the surface, so that attempts toward women's solidarity do not erase the specific testimony of African American women.

Another moment of critical difference occurs when Hutchins and McCauley describe the experience of rape:

JEANNIE: (*Curled up on bench*)
> To be raped is not to scream
> but to whimper and lock and never to remember
> but feel the closing in the thighs
> between the legs locking up everything
> biting lips, the teeth bleed.

ROBBIE: On the plantation you hafta stay tough and tight no matter how many times they come down there. Sally stayed down there with us in the quarters and at night they pulled us out in the dirt.[59]

Hutchins follows with, "In a rape crisis center, your wounds are fresh. They can put warm clothes on you, tell you it's not your fault." McCauley later responds that there "ain't no rape crisis center on the plantation."[60] As horrible as the experience of rape is, as Hutchins describes it, there is a moment when the survivor, at least today, can find some connection to a community in a rape crisis center. However, it would have been more historically accurate to note that there were no rape crisis centers until recently, and in that way, women, whatever their race or socioeconomic status, were furthered traumatized by the isolation imposed on them through the problematic, victim-blaming, cultural response to rape.

When trying to lead the audience into an active engagement with history and the importance of considering the impact of that history on the material lives of all individuals bearing its legacy, McCauley does allow herself distance from the character of Sally, as seen in moments such as the one described previously, when she alludes to her naked body as an issue that must be moved beyond. However, when she explores the tricky emotional territory involving the multigenerational aftermath of trauma, it becomes difficult not to "lose herself in character."

McCauley turns to her own inner experience to reconstruct a psychic self that has been left outside dominant representations but is part of the legacy of the traumatic history of interracial rape. "There are places in extreme," she explains: "places in between, there are places around, but we get stuck in the inside of sexual images and the way we internalize what we're supposed to do and what we're not supposed to do. Part of my struggle is around those issues of having been raped and silent about it. I know that information, I've dealt with it and I carry it with me. But in Sally's Rape, I found out more information about the tightness between my thighs."[61]

In Sally's Rape, McCauley and Hutchins come together to create a new public space and a new kind of interracial encounter in public space. This new encounter acknowledges the complex interface between the bodily experience of traumatic memory and the cultural inscription of identity onto the body. Within the performance, it becomes crucial to distinguish the trauma-induced silence from the silence imposed by the reproduction of stereotypes that suppress the expression of the traumatized subject.

McCauley joins writers such as Toni Morrison, Sherley Anne Williams, and Gayl Jones who reconstruct traumatized female ancestral figures from memory, imagination, and desire, and in the aesthetic space of multicultural writing and performance, the body and voice of the female ancestor and the contemporary woman join together to create a new form of testimony. This testimony attests to the paradox of traumatic memory, a memory that is both constantly present and absent within a survivor. The writer addresses the threat of violence felt by subordinated subjects and the way this threat operates at the level of memory, particularly traumatic memory that seizes or possesses the living body and testifies to violence against bodies in the past. The source of these bodily memories has been elided within dominant representations. Recovering the stories behind the residual sense involves a process of reconstruction and invention, reuniting the original body with a voice in which to speak the experience.

In "Focus on the Body: Pain, Praxis, and Pleasure in Feminist Performance," Jeanie Forte suggests that pain and live performance are "two cases when the body must be acknowledged, when it becomes visible/palpable through inhabiting temporally a process that depends fundamentally on its presence."[62] As McCauley stands naked on the auction block, she begins to describe the experience of being raped on the plantation and her feelings of deep, visceral connection to that history. She refers to "A TIGHTNESS BETWEEN HER THIGHS," bringing together the corporeal with a voice that speaks out and presenting a consciousness where there once was only an object. She describes the dreams in which Sally's pain haunts her, overcomes her:

> In the dream I. I am Sally being (*An involuntary sound of pain*)
> b'ah. Bein' bein' I . . . I being bound down I didn't I didn't wann be
> in the dream, bound down in the dream I am I am Sally being done
> it to I am down on the ground being done it to bound down didn't
> wanna be bound down on the ground. In the dream I am Sally
> down on the ground being done it to. In the dream I am Sally being
> done it to bound down on the ground.[63]

McCauley describes nightmares that function as traumatic intrusions, interrupting her sleep in the present and forcing her into the violence of the past.

McCauley uses her body as a source of information, tapping into a forgotten history that has left only the residue of complicated emotions. Shame and guilt, the emotions most frequently associated with traumatic histories, are, according to McCauley, "distortions of information and of the materials that we are living with. When the material of our past turns into shame and guilt, we stop talking about it, and it gets bigger and bigger and more distorted."[64] According to McCauley, these overwhelming emotions become manageable when they are identified as information to be understood within a particular historical and social context: "In the piece, I say, 'There's a tension between her thighs. When it lets go, she screams with terror.' So there's no good sex in there. Knowing that, the discovery of that power is something you can take with you as information, and let go. Whatever you want to do with what you let go is your business."[65] The terror does not remain in the isolated realm of traumatic reenactment. Instead, the mystery is named, and the bodily memories are placed within the context of the original traumatic experience.

In an interview with Vivian Patraka, McCauley suggests that "the mind and the body have to work together in order to create political theatre."[66] Later in the interview she elaborates on the body as a resource for performance material: "We carry in our bodies unspoken sadness and anger and resentment. It is bigger and harder to carry it than to release it. And when we realize it, we find out more information about it; we help our ability to move with it. You don't get rid of it, but you're able to handle it, take it with you, and to transform."[67] She goes on to say, "Pain is full of information. It exercises my mind to deal with that information. Again, it goes back to the body, the release. What you know is something you can carry with you rather than be burdened by."[68] Listening to her body, McCauley's performance tries to find a language for the voice she hears. It involves the struggle for the translation of traumatic experience that requires more than a single speaker.

McCauley is also interested in the process of forgetting or refusing to remember, in cultural amnesia and the price we pay for it in our daily living. Elin Diamond describes this focus:

> In her "history not remembered," McCauley follows Benjamin and Proust in demonstrating that voluntary memory—memory at the service of consciousness or intellect, whose function is to filter out disturbing memory traces—always falls short. It is only experience as it arises involuntarily, through mimetic associations, through unguarded correspondences, that can deliver the meaning of unremembered shocks. It's the historical richness of experience, of history as experience, that McCauley longs for.[69]

The "history not remembered" is the traumatic experience that haunts the body. Memory goes "underground," submerged in the body as the self loses its solid boundaries. Although traumatic memory initially becomes buried in the body to protect the survivor, it ultimately undermines. The same is true for the cultural memory of violence that becomes embedded in black and white bodies, only to be triggered or reenacted through interactions between those bodies.

In McCauley's performance, the voice that has been long silenced through trauma erupts: "I I I become others inside me, standing at the bus stop with my socks rolled down screaming things I shoulda said, 'Just because people are crazy don't mean they can't think straight!' Hollering periodically at white men 'YOU RAPED ME! GODDAMN MOTHERFUKA! YOU RAPED ME!'[70] McCauley's body is taken over by the voice of the unspeakable as she experiences the rage that has been denied an outlet. At this moment, her performance testifies to the delay in bodily response that is a fundamental feature of the traumatic experience. As

Bakare-Yusuf points out, there is an "erasure of human voice," but perhaps it is more accurate to state that the voice becomes displaced, or it loses its claim within the moment of experience and exists in search of another moment to express the pain. Cathy Caruth describes this phenomenon: "The event is not assimilated or experienced fully at the time, but only belatedly, in its repeated possession of the one who experiences it."[71] In the scene, the past takes possession of McCauley's body. Yelling at an indifferent crowd, she finds herself taken over by "others inside." The voices come forward at a moment of waiting in public space, trying to move forward and to have their impact on contemporary and future life.

Michel de Certeau's observation that "memory is a sort of anti-museum: it is not localizable" resonates in *Sally's Rape*.[72] There is no easy transition between the pain of history and the pain of today. The "pain [that] is full of information" transcends boundaries, including the boundaries of the body as it erupts forth, spilling over at unpredictable moments. McCauley moves continually between historical contexts to scenes such as "Trying to Transform," in which she becomes overwhelmed by the weight of the pain she carries and begins to yell at strangers at a bus stop. The bus stop figures as an interesting place within the U.S. history of race relations. The site of a rebellion that spurred on the Civil Rights Movement, it provides a connection to the other moments of awakening to and confrontation with white supremacy. Just like the library in 1964, the year the Civil Rights Act was enacted, the bus stop is a public space in need of transformation. McCauley takes these moments, icons, or sites of resistance and prevents them from remaining static representations of resistance. Instead, she inserts the unspeakable history of sexual violence within these spaces, altering them with the presence of the body and voice rising out of traumatic experience.

Standing at the bus stop, screaming about rape, McCauley forces into light the issue that trauma, like de Certeau's comment on memory, "is not localizable." Even the more recent understanding of the post-traumatic condition fails to account for the complex interplay between struggles in a hostile present environment and a past that keeps resurfacing. Maria Root suggests that the current understanding of traumatic stress

> does not necessarily reflect the reality of White women or women of colors' lives wherein many of the traumas affecting women are common, repeated, and current. These traumas include contextual threats through the interplay of domination by gender or race or

ethnicity that threaten the safety, limit the mobility, and denigrate the self-worth of an individual by virtue of a status she is born into. Even the notion of "post"-trauma responding largely originates in the White male experience of time-limited events, often singular in nature versus the prolonged, everyday effects of rape, and sexual and physical assault.[73]

Gerda Lerner refers to the rape of black women as "a weapon of terror."[74] In the interview with Patraka, McCauley describes the lasting effects of this chronic assault on the psychic integrity of African American women. Patraka compares the way in which "abused children become careful readers of people, responsive to the slightest shift in their behavior and mood, all of which are actually unpredictable" with McCauley's discussion of racism, which "is full of unpredictable violence, and one has to make up a code of behavior, of having papers, of giving the right signals to ward off the dangers when ultimately," in the words of McCauley, "there's nothing you can do."[75] It is this reality that is addressed within *Sally's Rape*.

This sense of overwhelming helplessness in the face of the legacy of racism as it is reenacted in the present is recognized in McCauley's performance, validating survivors and countering socially produced trauma. In *Sally's Rape*, McCauley produces what Julie Salverson speaks of as "a climate of witnessing," which, she says, "involves not only listening to someone's story, but allowing our attitudes and behaviors to be changed by it."[76] The performance allows bodies to come together to process information that can only be understood as within an intersubjective dynamic, a relationship, or a "reciprocal reflection" between women.

In the next chapter, this relationship between women and generations is complicated by a daughter's crisis around reproducing family testimony.

4 / Uncanny Spaces: Trauma, Cultural Memory, and Female Body in Gayl Jones's *Corregidora*

In "Truth and Testimony: The Process and the Struggle," Dori Laub describes his experience with the Holocaust-survivor testimony on which he bases his theories about witnessing and recovery: "survivors did not only need to survive so that they could tell their stories; they also needed to tell their stories in order to survive. There is, in each survivor, an imperative need to tell and thus to come to know one's story, unimpeded by ghosts from the past against which one has to protect oneself. One has to know one's buried truth in order to be able to live one's life."[1] Feminist inquiry has also held recovering narratives, or reclaiming "buried" or marginalized truths by and about women, as a fundamental concern. These "ghosts," literary or artistic foremothers such as described by Virginia Woolf in *A Room of One's Own* or Alice Walker in "In Search of Our Mother's Gardens," impede only when left unacknowledged, the lack of a connection to a creative lineage creating what Gilbert and Gubar notably refer to as an "anxiety of authorship" for female authors. Filmmaker Trinh T. Minh-ha's "Grandma's Story" chapter in *Woman, Native, Other* looks at the imperative of each generation to claim the cultural narrative of the female ancestor and suggests that the repetition of the story fulfills both giver and receiver, giving them a sense of "pleasure in the copy."[2] Specifically, she performs a cross-cultural feminist analysis that includes Gayl Jones's *Corregidora*, suggesting that the novel illustrates the female artist's compelling and pleasurable engagement with bearing witness through repetition. Indeed, at the end of *Dessa Rose*, Sherley Anne Williams reinforces this perspective when her protagonist, Dessa, describes finding an audience for her trauma narrative in the storytellers of future generations. In *Sally's Rape*, Robbie McCauley addresses the damage that occurs when these stories remain hidden or denied within the public sphere. However, in *Corregidora*, the "copy" passed down includes narratives fixed within a cultural framework that implicates the female body in its own trauma. Reproduction is not associated with pleasure here; rather, pleasure is linked to the disruption of narratives that inscribe the female body with the mark of trauma and with the recognition of traumatic memory in its multiple forms.

Corregidora provides insight into connections between narrative reproduction and traumatic repetition, beginning with a crisis related to the reproductive body that symbolizes this connection. Ursa Corregidora, the protagonist in *Corregidora*, loses the ability to bear children after her husband pushes her down a flight of stairs, resulting in an emergency hysterectomy. The opening crisis signals a shift in the connection between the female body, traumatic repetition, and narrative reproduction that this chapter hopes to illuminate, and new possibilities for testimony follow that attempt to release the protagonist's body from the collective anxiety projected onto it, a culturally produced repetition of the original trauma.

In "Trauma and Its Challenge to Society," Alexander McFarlane and Bessel van der Kolk assert that "conflicts between victims' and the bystanders' assessment of the meaning of trauma may set the stage for the trauma to be perpetuated in a larger social setting; soon the allocation of blame and not the trauma itself, may become the central issue."[3] *Corregidora* confronts traumatic repetition as it has been "perpetuated in a larger social setting" and in individual lives. Recovery here involves a renewed connection between body and voice. The protagonist, Ursa, creates narratives and performances that recognize the ways in which the body functions as speech and text, both discursively as a site of cultural inscription and as the locus of traumatic response. In doing so, she locates her own experience in relation to the bodies of the past and activates multiple levels of witness, including bearing witness to the intersubjective dynamic of witnessing itself, demonstrating that "the crucial if unstable difference between retraumatization and cure may be the difference between the unwitnessed and witnessed repetition: a repetition addressed to and heard by another becomes testimonial."[4] Recognizing the gaps in consciousness created by trauma, Jones uses the body strategically to indicate the limits of language, particularly in relation to expressing post-traumatic experience and acknowledging the uncanny figures of female sexuality inherited through the false testimony of patriarchal cultures. The new testimony intervenes by writing trauma, which "involves processes of acting out, working over, and to some extent working through in analyzing and 'giving voice' to the past,"[5] and using the body as a vehicle to express what remains outside conventional narrative. Jones uses illness or accident to indicate a period of transformation and transition. When Ursa performs her "New World Song" as a blues singer, she "gives voice" to the past, using her own body and fantasy constructions to disrupt sterile narratives that scapegoat the female body and individual women.

According to Cathy Caruth, "the belated experience of trauma . . . suggests that history is not only the passing on of a crisis, but also the passing on of a survival that can only be possessed within a history larger than any single individual or any single generation."[6] Caruth's comments on the belated experience of trauma indicate aspects of the experience that cannot be understood or lived immediately. It may take generations to understand more completely the implications of the traumatic experience. In this context, the *Corregidora* women's desire to "make generations" to tell the story signifies a recognition that the truth or evidence of their past can emerge only belatedly, through the voice and bodies of their kin. Jones offers perspectives on this belatedness through Ursa's search for meaning several generations beyond the initial crisis and her struggle to understand the experience of survival inherited by contemporary bodies. Ursa must first sort through the residues of traumatic experience as they exist within the cultural and familial framework and confront the process through which they have integrated the resulting cultural narratives into her own self-image as a young woman.

The transmission of family stories provides insight into the relationship between collective trauma and individual lives. Although the survivor's experience fractures his or her sense of a coherent self, leaving him or her stranded outside a symbolic order on which any community defines itself, it compels the survivor toward expression. A survivor-based account, a testimony, includes the struggle to find a language, and recent scholarship on transgenerational trauma posits that this struggle passes down within families. Kathleen Olympia Nadar observes in her article "Violence: Effects of Parents' Previous Trauma on Currently Traumatized Children" that "from transgenerational transmission [of trauma] described in the oral and written traditions of several cultures, it appears that experiences that occur with intensity—positive or negative—are imprinted on the parent or family in such a way that they emerge in subsequent generations."[7] According to Maria Root, this "imprinting" includes bodily responses and "the transmission of unresolved trauma and attendant defensive behaviors and/or helplessness that is transmitted transgenerationally as the result of an ancestor's direct trauma."[8] Both Nadar and Root suggest that subsequent generations pass on the experience through the transmission of narrative memory, or family stories, and through responses and behaviors that, since they reveal "unresolved trauma," may contradict or exceed the narrative.

While trauma survivors struggle with the inadequacy of language to express their experience, the crisis and its aftermath occur within a particular cultural framework, "culturally constructed landscapes of memory, the metaphoric terrain that shapes the distance and effort required to remember affectively charged and socially defined events that initially may be vague, impressionistic, or simply absent from memory."[9] These landscapes define the gaps and silences of traumatic memory and configure them within discursive norms. Alternative meanings remain within the survivor, who reenacts them in his or her daily life and must struggle to account for aspects of his or her experience that the dominant cultural framework has screened out. Nicholas Abraham refers to this memory as a kind of haunting in which "the phantom is a formation of the unconscious that has never been conscious—for good reason. It passes—in a way yet to be determined—from the parent's unconscious to the child's."[10] "What haunts," Abraham writes, "are not the dead, but the gaps left within us by the secrets of others."[11] Indeed, the protagonists must negotiate these gaps, through which they reenact the shock or void of signification produced by the original trauma and repeated in the psychic lives of subsequent generations.

In *Corregidora*, the trauma of the female ancestor occurs during a historical period of collective crisis. Ursa's Great Gram faces blame for exposing her community to the threat of death or to actual death in relation to outside forces. As Gayle Rubin points out, sexuality acquires an aura of danger in times of crisis: "Disputes over sexual behavior often become the vehicle for displacing social anxieties, and discharging their attendant emotional intensity."[12] Female sexuality evokes collective anxiety immediately following the crisis and as the story passes down to subsequent generations. The narrative inherited by the protagonist suggests that female sexuality poses a threat to the individual woman, her lovers, her family, and the community.

The violent events that haunt Ursa occurred during legal slavery and colonialism on a Brazilian coffee plantation. Ursa's great-grandmother, the "coffee-bean woman," tells story after story linking women's sexuality to death. As Elizabeth Swanson Goldberg suggests, "Situation within this historical context, female sexuality in *Corregidora* is contoured around the institutionalized rape of Ursa's great grandmother and grandmother, . . . originary violence which produced an incestuous line of women unable to conceive of sexuality apart from this violence."[13] If any man from Great Gram's own community took an interest in her, he risked his life, and the story of the young runaway who speaks to her in the field demonstrates this ugly fact. The encounter is innocent: "Wasn't nothing but seventeen. Couldn't have been more than seventeen or eighteen. And he had this dream he told me about. That was all he wanted me for, was to tell me about this dream."[14] However, Corregidora interrogates her about the young man, telling her that he has sent men to catch the youth. As Corregidora seizes her body, regaining control of her through rape, she imagines the young man's desperate attempt to escape: "And then somehow it got in my mind that each time [Corregidora] kept going down in me would be that boy's feets running. And then when he come, it meant they caught him."[15] Feeling complicit, she imagines her body as a conduit of death, and this connection between sexuality and destruction continues to shape the inner life of the Corregidora women long after slavery ends.

"Public events," explains Laura Brown, "visible to all, rarely themselves harbingers of stigma for their victims, things that can and do happen to men, all of these constitute trauma in the official lexicon. Their victims are rarely blamed for these events."[16] These public events, as Brown argues, include war and natural disaster and not the intimate violence suffered by the women in the text. The violation of the coffee-bean woman and her daughter occurs in private spaces, or rather the experience of the violated women remains a private, voiceless phenomenon. Their stories enter public discourse, however, through punishment and a spectacle of suffering for those involved with the woman. In *Corregidora*, the slave women's resistance against rape meets with a brutal display of power. Great Gram testifies, "they might wont your pussy, but if you do anything to get back at them, it'll be your life they be wonting, and then they make even that some kind of sex show, all them beatings and killings wasn't nothing but sex circuses, and all the white peoples, mens, womens, and childrens crowding around to see."[17] The exploited female body emerges as the readable text from the scene of the traumatic event, silenced in public but resonating with traumatic shock in the intimate core of her being. Through these public scenes and family secrets, the female body becomes marked within the cultural script as the bearer of traumatic instability.

In the stories, the female body harbors death, and through the repetition of the stories, she continues to threaten and warn. The stories illustrate the way in which women and death or trauma, the threat of death, occupy the same space in patriarchal discourse; they both embody the negation, the lack, that has been perceived as a menacing opposite to the phallus. Women's bodies signify the uncanny qualities of traumatic experience, which includes losing the filter that screens out the inevitable mortality; to be traumatized is to be feminized. The women's bodies, as uncanny objects, invoke fear and dread; their threat involves the surfacing (or resurfacing) of something hidden or repressed. Freud defines the uncanny as "that class of the frightening which leads back to what is known of old and long familiar."[18] In Freud's essay on the uncanny he defines the "familiar made strange" by referring to the maternal body. The uncanny as Freud describes it evokes fear; it threatens because it involves the resurfacing of something hidden or repressed, a connection with the mother's body that also suggests the destabilization of a coherent self. The symbolic order defines itself against this space. Death and sex work together to threaten the individual or communal sense of wholeness, stability, or strength.

Feminist revisions of Freud's theory about the uncanny shift the emphasis away from the acceptance of the uncanny nature of women's bodies and toward an analysis of the misogynistic assumptions forwarded by this reading. Elisabeth Bronfen redefines the uncanny as that which "always entails anxieties about fragmentation, about the disruption or destruction of any narcissistically informed sense of personal stability, bodily integrity, immortal individuality."[19] According to Bronfen, the anxiety evoked by the maternal body stems from the fear of death and not only the loss of the phallus. The female body, therefore, becomes associated with death and not just sexual difference:

To be precise, what the phallus, as the privileged signifier for patriarchal notions of potency, ultimately screens out, is a recognition of death. Under the aegis of the phallus, culture can insist on the concepts of immortality by deflecting notions of mortality, in a "press for translation" on to the feminine body, sexualising them in the image of the castrated or demonic Woman, who as the feminine equivalent of the phallic masculine subject, harbours the denied recognition of death.[20]

Corregidora's coffee-bean woman becomes the "castrated or demonic Woman" within the cultural narratives that contain traumatic experience, and stories about reproductive lives reinforce the status as a threatening figure. The stories are passed down even by female relatives, who align the body with supernatural, uncanny powers, reflecting the internalization and perpetuation of this cultural message, and through this narrative reproduction, female sexuality becomes the "familiar made strange." Collective memory inscribes trauma on the female body, thus containing trauma within this inscription, a strategy that delays indefinitely a direct confrontation with human vulnerability. Represented by some sexual other, death anxiety can be articulated without infecting or destabilizing the patriarchal order. The female body provides the site for the struggle against the threat of ego dissolution, since woman functions symbolically as the embodiment of precariousness.

The silence and the repetition encountered in relation to the stories of the female body's violation represent a bodily performance of traumatic memory. Traumatic memory often alternates between silence and uncontrollable repetition. In *Corregidora*, the survivors' voices repeat the same story, creating paradoxically a kind of noisy silence for Ursa. The repetition both overwhelms and numbs Ursa, and she too must search beyond the story she has been told to locate its meaning in her own life.

The uncanny force, the "buried truth" or what Freud referred to as "everything that ought to have remained . . . secret and hidden but has come to light,"[21] does not remain hidden in the texts. Female relatives resurrect the ghosts, confirming Dori Laub's claim that "one has to know one's buried truth in order to be able to live one's life."[22] In the space of Ursa's own imagination, she repeatedly addresses the coffee-bean woman, fleshing out the slave woman's subjectivity, violated in life and erased in history. Ursa learns to listen to the language of ghosts, who exist within the bodies of the living, transmitting memory through these bodies.

Ursa searches to find a language for implicit memory and the place of the body in testimony. Part of the task of moving away from the false projection of cultural anxiety onto femininity entails acknowledging the actual bodily experience of trauma, or telling the body's story, instead of inscribing a story onto the body. Ursa uses her body/memory to construct an alternative testimony, identifying and differentiating the way in which the female body functions in narratives of crisis from the actual experience of that crisis. It is through this creation of a new form of testimony, one that acknowledges the body's voice and the changing complexity of the traumatic response as it resonates within new bodies, in new places, that traumatic repetition loosens its paralyzing grip.

In the patriarchal culture, these stories function within what Sandra Lee Bartky has called a "pedagogy of shame" that instructs young girls about the inherent danger and corruption of their bodies. Not directly connected to specific actions, the experience of shame and guilt in relation to their bodies and sexuality stems from the female socialization process in which girls are taught "to internalize the gaze of . . . a 'hostile witness' to our bodily being."[23] Bartky suggests that "to the extent that we so often accept the lesser lives that are offered us, and insofar as we internalize intimations of inferiority, we must assume that the inculcation of shame and guilt in women is a pervasive feature of social life."[24] In the case of *Corregidora,* the trauma narratives fail to create a true witness. No real address, the exchange between survivor and her witness, appears from the telling of the stories. Rather, the witness turns inward and the psychic isolation this creates repeats or copies the initial traumatic response and undermines testimony. The novel provides insight into the intimate effects of these trauma narratives on the daughters of the first-generation survivors.

Ursa's sexuality has been shaped in her childhood as a captive audience to the sexual terror of Corregidora, the Brazilian plantation owner who raped her great-grandmother and grandmother, his own biological child. Ursa's inheritance of her foremothers' beauty forces her to struggle constantly with those who would possess her. Jones provides the reader with many descriptions of Ursa's physical appearance and her attractiveness. Throughout the novel, there are constant reminders of Ursa's sexual desirability. In every interaction, she must see herself as an object of someone else's desire or as a sexual threat to other women. In both the public space of the nightclub, the fair, and the town streets and in the private spaces in which she seeks refuge and recovery, Ursa's body exists as a spectacle, revealing a legacy that she has internalized and that is confirmed by the outside world. With no relief in either private or public life, Ursa feels overwhelmed by a sense of imminent danger related to sexuality. Her sexuality defines her essentially, and very little space exists for other aspects of her subjectivity. The legacy of Corregidora's plantation follows her, and she seems enslaved to others and owned by their desires.

One of the early dream-memory moments in the novel involves Ursa's sexual experimentation as a child. Her mother sees Ursa's friend Henry look up her dress and then calls out to Ursa to return home. Once inside, her mother scolds her. Immediately following the specific memory, another voice utters, "I bet you were fucking before I was born. Before you was a thought." Her thoughts answer, "I got evil in me. Corregidora's evil. Ole man, he just kept rolling." The voice appears to offer a response to the first memory, suggesting that for Ursa even an innocent moment from childhood has been tainted by the Corregidora legacy. "I have a birthmark between my legs," Ursa reminds herself later.[25] Ursa's husband, Mutt, sensing the ghosts that haunt the space of their intimacy, pleads with her to put some distance between their lives and their painful family history: "'Don't look like that, Ursa,' he had said and pulled me toward him, 'Whichever way you look at it, we ain't them.'" She cannot respond affirmatively: "I didn't answer that, because the way I'd been brought up, it was almost as if I was."[26] While she feels she carries the mark of Corregidora, Ursa cannot feel her own sexuality. She experiences the numbing effects of trauma. During her sexual encounters with Mutt and Tadpole, her body performs, but the rest of her remains at a distance, removed from the intimacy. The sexual games Mutt plays with Ursa mirror the paradoxical obsession with and detachment from sex that has affected their married life.

The dynamic between Mutt and Ursa begins to reflect Ursa's family history. Mutt's possessiveness consumes him as he watches the male audience members respond to Ursa when she sings onstage. He refuses to make love with her at home but brings her to a fair and forces her to dance provocatively with him in front of others at the fair. Rubbing against Ursa, aware of the eyes of strangers with a pornographic self-consciousness, he creates a public performance of their sexuality. Although Mutt's performance appears to perpetrate a cruel act that reinforces the connection between intimacy and violation, it can be interpreted as a more complicated reaction to the problems within their private life. He simply forces Ursa to see others watching them. Their lovemaking always has a sense of being watched, as Corregidora haunts the space between their bodies and taints their intimacy.

Ursa worries that the story will remain trapped within her now that she can no longer "make generations" to bear witness to the horrors of Brazilian slavery. Corregidora has infected her inner life so completely that she even attributes the fall that leaves her unable to reproduce to his desire to thwart her efforts to pass on the story: "Even my clenched fists couldn't stop the fall. That old man still howls inside me. . . . My veins are centuries meeting."[27] Corregidora, the perpetrator of unspeakable crimes against the human soul, looms large in Ursa's psyche. Even the blood within her veins divides her. Both victim and abuser exist within her frame. She feels connected beyond her control to the story of her family: "Consequences. It seems as if you're not singing the past, you're humming it. Consequences of what? Shit, we're all consequences of something. Stained with another's past as well as our own. Their past in my blood. I'm a blood. Are you mine, Ursa, or theirs?"[28] The stain marks her body, and "consequences" implies the sense of guilt she has internalized as a Corregidora woman. Ursa needs to engage in the strategies of recognition suggested by Bronfen in her revising of Freud's "uncanny," so that she can exorcize the "demonic woman" from her psyche, freeing herself from this projection of patriarchal anxiety.

Since for the Corregidora women there is nowhere to express their pain in the outside world, they keep it to themselves, repeatedly telling their stories within the confines of their own home. The trauma remains a part of their inner world, separate from the public space hostile to the female body. Although they tell the story in an effort to preserve the "evidence" that would exonerate them, the space in which they contain their testimony creates a painful rift within the psyche of their granddaughter, who has inherited both the story and its private telling, which functions as a kind of pedagogy of shame for her. She takes with her into the public sphere a secret knowledge of her family and therefore of herself. After the accident, she struggles with the internal witness created by this dichotomy, struggling to form a testimony that incorporates the complexity of her experience.

The "demonic woman" becomes a hostile internal witness who appears in her dreams. These dreams contain vivid scenes that portray the female body as a demonic force that reproduces its corruption and instability. Dreams reveal the internalization of the fear of the female body as contaminated with death. In dreams, Ursa gives birth to monsters incompatible with life, or she becomes one herself, almost involuntarily destroying life around her.

Ursa struggles to incorporate the sexual abuse experienced directly by her great-grandmother and grandmother and suffers from a trauma linked both to her family's past and her present condition as a woman. In her dreams, too, the traumatic family history repeats itself, as Corregidora's body fills her in every aspect of procreation, both in sex and in birth:

I dreamed that my belly was swollen and restless, and I lay without moving, gave birth without struggle, without feeling. But my eyes never turned to my feet. I never saw what squatted between my knees. But I felt the humming and beating of wings and claws in my thighs. And I felt a stiff penis inside me. "Those who have fucked their daughters would not hesitate to fuck their own mothers." Who are you? What have I born? His hair was like white wings, and we were united at birth.[29]

Ursa's dream suggests that she fears she will continue to function as a vessel for Corregidora's evil. She has internalized the message that her body carries this uncanny force, a supernatural, demonic quality rendering the familiar strange. Her body reproduces also the source of its own suffering. She gives birth disconnected from her body and "without feeling," unable to register the experience tactually or visually. She only senses the violation of a "stiff penis inside" and the voice that names the violation. The union, or reunion, that occurs at birth traps her in a cycle of pain, and her body's seeming complicity threatens her psychic integrity.

The text disrupts the culturally produced link between femininity and trauma by using physical illness to represent a movement through uncanny spaces, thus showing the spaces as transitory and not fixed or essentialized. If Freud's earlier rendition of the uncanny included a dread related to the blurred boundaries between life and death, and projected this dread onto the female form, *Corregidora* transforms this cultural narrative by representing the uncanny as a rejuvenative, liminal state. Although the body has been seized in narrative and traumatic memory, the text uses illness and the rest associated with it as a kind of gestational period, fluid and dynamic, through which a new body passes. Illness functions as transformation, and in these states of sickness and recuperation, Ursa explores other possibilities of representation.

As Gloria Anzaldúa describes in *Borderlands/La Frontera: The New Mestiza,* a by-product of being "pushed out of the tribe," or what Maria Root refers to as "insidious trauma," is a heightened artistic perception and drive to create meaning from the chaos, to express the experience of the borderlands, which Anzaldúa refers to as the "Coatlicue state."[30] In *Corregidora*, the female protagonist passes through a borderlands when an accident compromises her bodily integrity and forces her into a period of physical rest. The Coatlicue state offers a reprieve from all forms of intimacy, including sexuality, allowing the individual to separate from others' demands on her body and to distinguish her own desire from the expectations of others. Ursa emerges from this period changed, with a new voice ready to testify. Ursa does more than repeat the stories handed down to her. She uncovers the unspoken truths omitted within the official archive of the event and seeks to reconstruct what she refers to as "private memory" to escape the all-consuming forces of a collective memory that aligns femininity with danger and instability.

Maria Root's description of insidious trauma includes the development of a keen sensitivity to environment. This altered awareness appears very similar to Anzaldúa's writings on the "Intimate Terrorism" in *Borderlands*, particularly the development of extrasensory perception, or *la facultad*. *La facultad*, as Anzaldúa explains, is an affective feature of individuals who have been rejected from or wounded within the group, those who no longer fit because their pain—their trauma—has isolated them and changed them permanently. Anzaldúa links this sense to the Coatlicue state, an uncanny place in which the individual must face all the uncertainty of being. "Living in a state of psychic unrest, in a Borderland," Anzaldúa writes, "is what makes poets write and artists create."[31] Traumatic experience causes one to pass through this borderland, which Anzaldúa also refers to as a "prelude to crossing."[32] The process corresponds to creative endeavors, to the creation of a testimony to express the crossing. Infected by the images of corrupt, dangerous female sexuality, Ursa must retreat into herself to disrupt the repetition of this narrative by creating new landscapes of memory. Since Ursa cannot change her physical environment, the new landscapes form in the altered state of illness and recovery. The Coatlicue state conjures or invokes implicit memory, a memory form that exists within the body in search of a language.

The new journey is very different from the original survivor's. Ursa needs silence first, to retreat from previous representation and the compulsion to repeat. Ursa struggles with feeling out of control of her own body and her life because of both accident and fate. When her husband pushes her down the stairs, she loses her ability to fulfill the wishes of her female ancestors to "make generations" to continue to bear witness to the story of their enslavement and sexual abuse. Deeply connected to her grandmothers' desire for her to create with her body a vehicle for memory, Ursa's sense of destiny and self-perception changes radically with the physical alteration. Ursa has significant gaps in her memory around the events of the accident. She does not remember her trip to the hospital clearly, which she and Tadpole discuss while he cares for her at his home. These memory gaps present a contrast with Ursa's sense of responsibility for preserving family history. She carries a photograph of the "mad Portuguese" slaveholder who fathered her grandmother and her mother, so she never forgets what he looks like. During her physical recovery from the accident, Ursa becomes haunted by dreams and thoughts of her grandmother and great-grandmother, and these flashbacks occur as italicized sections interspersed throughout the novel. The interruptions in the linear narrative appear as inner dialogues and direct memories of specific events. They also involve a preoccupation with memory itself and the act of remembering; Ursa becomes focused on recalling her grandmother's remembering. The novel, in large part, explores the memory process, including the inheritance of both specific memories and a style of remembering.

According to Robert Jay Lifton, "the struggle in the post-traumatic experience is to reconstitute the self into the single self, reintegrate itself. And it's in that combination of feeling and not feeling, that the creative aspect of the survivor experience, or the potentially illuminating aspect of the survivor experience, takes shape."[33] This space of "feeling and not feeling" is a kind of borderlands, like the Coatlicue state described by Anzaldúa and through which Ursa passes. The reconstituted self that emerges from this transitional space must have addressed the competing, often contradictory discourses at work in relation to the displacement from both the site of the original trauma and dominant cultural forces.

In *Corregidora*, the reintegration includes what Lifton refers to as "the creative aspect of the survivor experience," which entails finding a form for the multiple, often paradoxical types of memory that inform the post-traumatic life. Through the Coatlicue state, Ursula invents imaginary spaces in which she can confront the inscription of her body as unstable, chaotic. When she leaves this transitional space, she must invent forms that allow for the creation of an address so that the internal witness, the one suffering from self-alienation caused by the pedagogy of shame, finds a voice for her own story. Laurence Kirmayer suggests that the challenge of moving from fantasy-like accountings, which may offer a more accurate rendering of the crisis of witnessing, to recognizable narrative structures is one of language: "their problem is not the limits of memory but of language—the inadequacy of ordinary words to express all they have witnessed."[34] The text seems to acknowledge the problems with using either pure fantasy or narrative realism to express the experience of survival. Instead, it moves between these forms, highlighting their distinctness while also allowing them to blend into each other. *Corregidora* shifts from first-person exterior narrative to interior dialogues with ghosts of the past.

Creative experiments become the basis for the public performance of new forms of testimony, which allows Ursa to be more fully in her own immediate present. Ursa desires to create and perform a "song branded with the new world," a public testimony that acknowledges the layered texture of her experience as a Corregidora woman. The publicness involves creating an address to include the original story and its effects on the lives of the women whose bodies and spirits bear its legacy. Ursa recognizes that she has been called on to perform as witness and that she needs to distinguish the voices of the past from the ideological renderings. Her testimony articulates the need to identify and to revise the stories used within the "pedagogy of shame." By investigating the transmission of testimony as it shapes identities across generations, the novel complicates the biological determinism that binds survivors by sex to a destiny of pain. *Corregidora* reveals that the corruption of bodily integrity is not inherent to female sexuality but instead becomes associated with femininity through the cultural marking of female sexuality and silencing the survivor's voice. Returning to the female body, to what Freud refers to again as the "unheimliche place . . . the entrance to the former Heim of all human beings, to the place where each of us lived once upon a time and in the beginning,"[35] Ursa seeks to transcend the fear and instability inscribed onto that body within patriarchal discourse. The text transforms traumatic memory from a spectacle of suffering to a dynamic performance of narrative, allowing the expression of past and present pain within collective and individual memory. Personal crisis becomes creative opportunity when Ursa uses her ability to form new testimonies and to bear witness to the process of witnessing itself.

In *Corregidora*, transformation begins by recognizing the bodily response within the process of remembering. In the first flashback, we are introduced to Ursa's great-grandmother and the stories she would recount about her sexual abuse under slavery: "It was as if the words were helping her, as if the words repeated again and again could be a substitute for memory, were somehow more than the memory."[36] Memory and words are connected here, but they are not one and the same. Memory becomes more than the narratives constructed through language and transmitted to listeners. Ursa recalls observing a process or performance of memory, a testimony wherein the words narrate not only a past event but the present conditions of the person reexperiencing the memory on some profound level. Shoshana Felman describes testimony as a performance that involves the body and voice: "to vow to tell, to promise and produce one's own speech as material evidence for truth—is to accomplish a speech act, rather than simply to formulate a statement."[37] In testimony, the survivor attempts to piece together the fragmented memory, to join the frozen, muted image with the body that has been appropriated by terror. Testimony of traumatic memory, therefore, involves the struggle to produce a language, a voice and form, that expresses the unknowable and unspeakable existing through the gaps in consciousness. Indeed, the struggle itself is an element of the testimony. This struggle for the production of a language to voice the previously unspeakable also constitutes a performance of memory that counters the temporal break caused by trauma.

The connection between body and memory appears throughout *Corregidora*. When Ursa returns home late in the novel, she watches Mama recounting one of Great Gram's stories, and the boundaries between performer and performed blur significantly: "It was as if she had more than learned it by heart, though. It was as if their memory, the memory of all the Corregidora women, was her memory too, as strong with her as her own private memory, or almost as strong. But now she was Mama again."[38] Ursa herself has been called on to give her body to the cause of preserving memory by "making generations." Her grandmother wants her to reproduce so that the story can be passed on. Other forms of physical evidence had been destroyed long ago, after slavery ended in Brazil, when "the officials burned all the papers cause they wanted to play like what had happened before never did happen."[39] Their situation is not unique, as Tadpole, Ursa's employer and future husband, tells her with his own family story of stolen property and destroyed records: "Nothing. Anyway, they ain't nothing you can do when they tear the pages out of the book and they ain't no record of it. They probably burned the pages."[40] The "evidence" of their violation would exist only through children in the reproduction of their bodies and their memory: "The important thing is making generations. They can burn the papers but they can't burn conscious, Ursa. And that's what makes the evidence. That's what makes the verdict."[41] This imperative could not be questioned, as Ursa discovers at a young age:

> "You telling the truth, Great Gram?"
> She slapped me.
> "When I'm telling you something you don't ever ask if I'm lying.

Because they didn't want to leave no evidence of what they done—
so it couldn't be held against them. And I'm leaving evidence.
And you got to leave evidence too. And your children got to leave
evidence. And when it come time to hold up the evidence, we got to
have evidence to hold up. That's why they burned all the papers, so
there wouldn't be no evidence to hold up against them."
    I was five years old then.[42]

Ursa remembers her grandmothers' story so vividly because they have
created a witness in her. The importance of making generations exists
not only in reproducing the narrative but also in reproducing the process
of bearing witness, or the witness and witness-listener dynamic, which
they created and repeatedly performed within their home.

    Dori Laub explains the role of the listener: "The emergence of the nar-
rative which is being listened to—and heard—is, therefore, the process
and the place wherein the cognizance, the 'knowing' of the event is given
birth to. The listener, therefore, is party to the creation of knowledge, de
novo. The testimony to the trauma thus includes its hearer, who is, so
to speak, the blank screen on which the event comes to be inscribed for
the first time."[43] Ursa functions as a "blank screen" on which the older
Corregidora women inscribe their testimony. Their home becomes a kind
of theater of witness. Without subsequent generations, the performance
cannot exist. *Corregidora* raises important questions about the impact of
the witnessing relationship on generations who inherit and function as a
witness to stories of trauma. Thus, Jones's narrative strategy of weaving
together Ursa's response to the accident and her memories of her role as
the witness-listener presents the complex psychic connections between
events. The narrative style reflects the layering effect of trauma.

    Janice Harris calls *Corregidora* an "uncompromising portrait of the
artist as a young woman,"[44] arguing that one should not neglect the development of Ursa's artistry by focusing on the psychological issues obvi-
ously present within the novel. However, it seems impossible to avoid the
connections between her music and her survival. The blues music performed by Ursa acts as a form of mourning and remembrance, stages in
recovery, according to Judith Herman. The change in Ursa's voice after the
accident reflects the alteration of her psyche. As Cat tells her, "it sounds
like you been through something."[45] At one point Ursa asks herself in an
interior monologue, "What do the blues do for you?" to which another
voice responds, "It helps me to explain what I can't explain."[46] Since she
can no longer rely on "making generations," she brings her story into

the public in her singing, and with the audience, she creates an address that includes all the pain, grief, and pleasure of her life: "Then let me give witness the only way I can. I'll make a fetus out of grounds of coffee to rub inside my eyes. When it's time to give witness, I'll make a fetus out of grounds of coffee. I'll stain their hands."[47] From the grounds of coffee—fragments that suggest the ashes of Great Gram, the coffee-bean woman, and the remains of the Brazilian coffee plantation—Ursa conceives a new song. Through her music, she finds a pure space in which she expresses a self that transcends the corruption of the Corregidora legacy: "I am Ursa Corregidora. I have tears for eyes. I was made to touch my past at an early age. I found it on my mother's tiddies. In her milk. Let no one pollute my music. I will dig out their temples. I will pluck out their eyes."[48] In her performance she finds a sense of bodily integrity. The "evidence" that was once trapped in the body of Corregidora women, only finding an outlet through the generations, now emerges as an address in public space. And in her live singing, the record she creates from this evidence is never the same. Through her performance, she bears witness to the act of witnessing itself, which is what she has had to survive as a Corregidora daughter listening to the stories repeated by her grandmothers.

The testimony Ursa struggles to create with her singing does not bear witness to the experience of her female ancestors alone. Rather, she must find a way to document her own experience, the legacy of the brutality that cannot be contained within one lifetime. She describes her desire to find a new form for her testimony:

> I wanted a song that would touch me, touch my life and theirs.
> A Portuguese song, but not a Portuguese song. A new world song.
> A song branded with the new world. I thought of a girl who had
> to sleep with her master and mistress. Her father, the master.
> Her father's daughter. The father of her daughter's daughter. How
> many generations? Days that were pages of hysteria. Their survival
> depended on suppressed hysteria. She went and got her daughter,
> womb swollen with the child of her own father. How many genera-
> tions had to bow to his genital fantasies? They were fisherman and
> planters. And you with the coffee-bean face, what were you? You
> were sacrificed. They knew you only by the signs of your sex.[49]

The blues offers an experimental form through which she can find respite from the direct testimony of her grandmothers. The music also allows her to express the other aspects of her inheritance: the emotional and behavioral legacy that she communicates to her audience. Onstage, singing lyrics dripping with sexual innuendo, Ursa creates a performance from her status as the irresistible object of desire. She stages the familiar story, her body before the male audience, seeming to invite them with her song. The responses she evokes become part of the performance, a drama of the dynamic into which she and the women in her family have been forced ever since the coffee-bean woman had her genitals examined on the auction block. Within the setting of the club, however, the male behavior is censured, as disruptive audience members face removal from the club. Her performance causes a shift in accountability, and the men must deal with the consequences of objectifying the female body.

Ursa's mother resists her singing because of the sexuality implicit in her lyrics. Instead Mama listens to gospel music, a form from which all hints of sexuality have been purged. Ursa does not seek to purify with her music. Rather, she tries to understand and explain: "Yes, if you understood me, Mama, you'd see I was trying to explain it, in blues, without words, the explanation somewhere behind the words. To explain what will always be there. Soot crying out my eyes. 'O Mister who comes to my house You do not come to visit You do not come to see me to visit You come to hear me sing with my thighs You come to see me open my door and sing with my thighs.'"[50]

The gospel music chosen by Ursa's mother offers a kind of cleansing and forgiveness, which Ursa does not seek. Instead, she wants to know and speak the truth of her feelings of survival. For Ursa, the public expression of her painful emotions provides a healing previously unknown to her. Her mother's gospel music assumes a higher authority. Ursa acknowledges only the power of her song to help her move a little closer to the truth of her own life.

The difference in Ursa's and her mother's preference for music reveals a greater gap between mother and daughter, specifically, in the way they cope with the legacy of Corregidora. In gospel music Mama finds absolution and a reprieve from her physical existence. She can deny her sexuality, painfully complicated as it is, and focus on the life of the spirit alone. Ursa senses Mama's effort to forget her own life and her own desire: "And when she talked, Mutt, it was like she had something else behind her eyes. Corregidora was easier than what she wouldn't tell me. They'd look at her. They'd tell theirs and then they'd look at her to bear them witness."[51] Ursa remembers, however, that Mama began questioning the testimony, trying to understand Corregidora's acts against the women: "How can it be? She was the only one who asked that question."[52] Ursa's memory of Mama's questioning leads her to ask about Mama's own life, the first life lived outside the physical bounds of slavery. The spiritual boundaries are much less clear, as Ursa discovers, and the past consumed her mother's own story.

Ursa asks, "How could she bear witness to what she'd never lived, and refuse me what she had lived?"[53] Her need to rebuild her past and release herself from traumatic memory begins with her mother's past, specifically the story of her parents' relationship and her birth: "I couldn't be satisfied until I had seen Mama, talked to her, until I had discovered her private memory."[54] Mama's private memory provides the possibility for Ursa to construct her own "new world song" to bear witness to the passing on of survival and to move beyond the repetition of Great Gram's and Gram's testimony.

If Ursa can determine that point in Mama's life, perhaps she can learn how to live her own life beyond the reproduction of the Corregidora narrative. During a visit home, Mama tells Ursa about her father, Martin, the man who called her mother Corey, the only time she is identified by her own name in the text.[55] The relationship of Ursa's parents was, like Ursa and Mutt's, also marked with a sense of being watched in their most intimate moments, of a sexuality that must perform before a desiring audience, but one that also does not approach real intimacy. The incident when Martin walks into his mother-in-law's room and finds the older woman powdering naked breasts demonstrates this repetition; Corey stands in the doorway, watching her husband staring at her mother, who is aware of both presences. Corey knows that her mother has helped to create the scene in the bedroom, yet her mother does nothing to cover her nudity. It is as if she prolongs the scene to give Corey long enough to absorb its content. Once again, Corey must perform as witness to her mother as an object of male desire. The scene also exposes Martin. Men are all ruled by their desire, Gram, Corey's mother, seems to want her to learn and to accept. To Martin, all Corregidora women are whores. This belief is confirmed later when he tears Corey's dress, forcing her to walk down the street half dressed. Once in the street, she finds herself being perceived as indecent, a Corregidora woman with her body displayed in the public space for all interested parties to evaluate and make their bids.

The exchange between Ursa and Mama again confirms that their sense of self, including their sexual identity, connects to a family history. Ursa wants to free her mother from the traumatic memory of her grandmothers. Mama's life, as Ursa sees it, has been blocked by the overwhelming responsibility toward the past. Mama's painful knowledge of her birth prevented her from developing her own sexuality, and this in turn, has affected Ursa's relationships. Ursa leaves Mama feeling less burdened : "I was thinking that now Mama had gotten it all out, her own memory—at least to me anyway—maybe she and some man . . . But then, I was thinking, what had I done about my own life?"[56] The grandmother's and great-grandmother's memory had subsumed Mama's memory, but now Ursa has a more direct link to an immediate history. Ursa finds strength and healing from her ability to act as a midwife to her mother's personal story, and in this moment she locates a critical difference between the collective memory of slavery, on a familial and communal level, and individual memory. This delivery allows Ursa to pursue the questions about her own life and to develop answers beyond the repetition of the Corregidora nightmare.

Corregidora's ending has drawn complex critical response. Bruce Simon argues that Ursa's return to Mutt signals "a return to trauma" and that "Ursa's attempt to address a listener, to give testimony, to bear witness, is literally interrupted" by what Simon refers to as the "compulsive repetitiveness" of the ending.[57] Madhu Dubey claims, however, that "Ursa's blues song . . . seeks to express a black feminine sexuality that can at once contain and transcend the contradictory history of American slavery."[58] As Marianne Hirsch suggests in her discussion of postmemory, artistic expression that acknowledges the original story while also expressing its shifting, transforming consequences in new contexts for new generations offers an antidote to traumatic repetition across generations. Artists replace the fixity of traumatic repetition by "displacing and recontextualizing these well-known images in their artistic work" and counter the devastating effects of repetition, providing a "mostly helpful vehicle of working through a traumatic past."[59] Ursa's reunion with Mutt offers the possibility of reintegrated sexuality, always informed by the traumatic past but now also expressed within Ursa's "new world song."

In *Corregidora*, the protagonist negotiates the meaning of the traumatized body that she has inherited. Again, if "what haunts are . . . the gaps left within us by the secrets of others,"[60] then as a haunted survivor, Ursa must return the gaps, the unspoken truths that have resulted in the compulsive repetition of reductive and damaging narratives about the female body. Although, as Judith Herman notes, "resolution of the trauma is never final; recovery is never complete,"[61] through the creative unmaking of the world, Ursa emerges to construct a new story away from a landscape of memory that implicates the female body in her own trauma. Rising from this Coatlicue space, Ursa reconstructs the story of traumatic experience, the testimony of her own life as a survivor, moving from fantasy forms to an address that incorporates all aspects of memory. Through Ursa's "new world song," transgenerational trauma finds at last a form and a voice.

The next chapter turns to Anna Deavere Smith, who also counters traumatic repetition and its painful legacies, inventing a kind of "new world" performance that replaces the monotonous, blank affect, image, and language of traumatic repetition with a productive dialogue of witness.

5 / "I Have Never Seen a Movie Like That": Traumatic Memory and the "Acceleration of History" in Anna Deavere Smith's *Twilight: Los Angeles, 1992*

> *Modern memory is, above all, archival. It relies entirely on the materiality of the trace, the immediacy of the recording, the visibility of the image. What began as writing ends as high fidelity and tape recording.*
> —PIERRE NORA, "BETWEEN MEMORY AND HISTORY:
> LES LIEUX DE MEMOIRE"

> *It was like the end of the world: the violence, the destruction, the terror. I have never seen a movie like that.*
> —ANNA DEAVERE SMITH, *TWILIGHT: LOS ANGELES, 1992*

The PBS production of Anna Deavere Smith's play *Twilight: Los Angeles, 1992* opens with the line quoted in the epigraph, which evokes the tension between Nora's observation on media-facilitated public memory and a belated, fractured post-traumatic response that, as Smith's interviewed subject expresses above, exceeds the representational boundaries. The comparison between an actual crisis and film images alludes to the dominant conception of memory as a photographic still[1] or a film engraved in consciousness to represent specific experience. Nora's claim suggests this conception's functioning on a cultural level, where visual images pervade the collective consciousness and shape the perception of events. "Indeed," Nora writes, "we have seen the tremendous dilation of our very mode of historical perception, which, with the help of the media, has substituted for a memory entwined in the intimacy of a collective heritage the ephemeral film of currents events."[2] This "ephemeral film" works within an "acceleration of history" and against pauses, breaks, and somatic resonances that mark the post-traumatic struggle for representation.[3]

In *Twilight: Los Angeles, 1992*,[4] Anna Deavere Smith explores problems and processes related to historical perception and personal memory around the Rodney King beating in Los Angeles. In the preceding chapters, the black female subject's attempts to transmit trauma testimony is always hindered by the discursive limits placed on her body. The evidence of her experience is always misread or tampered with by an "expert," authority figure, or institution such Cuvier, Nehemiah, the university, the courtroom, or the library, with each figure or entity attempting to fix the testimony's meaning within the discursive limits of a specific racial hegemony. In Smith's work, she inserts the black female body at the site of transmission to serve as an agent against this effort and toward a greater accountability to the survivor. Her work includes performing all stages in the witnessing encounter: the survivor, the witness-listener, and the process itself. Smith's play negotiates the intersection between history and memory, the point at which memory, still dynamic and fluid, meets history's media-ation: the totalizing schema comprising "the materiality of the trace, the immediacy of the recording, the visibility of the image." The play explores the points at which crisis and memory's response to it exceeds known narrative structures. Creating a space in which the meaning of memory lingers unsettled, *Twilight* resists the acceleration of history, specifically in relation to the forces of media and civil authority moving quickly to seal the incident within a dominant, racialized frame.

Nora writes that "representation proceeds by strategic highlighting, selecting samples and multiplying examples. Ours is an intensely retinal and powerfully televisual memory,"[5] invoking the dominant modern conception about memory as photographic still when it meets with the rapidly moving force of visual technology. The transition between spontaneous memory and history involves highlighting, selecting, and multiplying according to dominant visual tropes to create a symbolic meaning, and "televisual memory" involves the acceleration of this process. Visual tropes participate in the construction of historical narrative or what Susan Stanford Friedman refers to in "Making History: Reflections on Feminism, Narrative, and Desire" as "the narrative of what has happened—[which] foregrounds the role of the narrator of past events and consequently the nature of narrative as a mode of knowing that selects, organizes, orders, interprets, and allegorizes."[6] *Twilight* looks at media[7] images and visual perception as they become vehicles of a dominant historical narrative that destroys intimate memory in its efforts to order, select, and organize. "The tremendous dilation of our very mode of historical perception" articulated through "the ephemeral film of currents events"[8] raises question about the power of media sources to shape the collective understanding of events, such as the trial related to the Rodney

King beating and the violent response to the verdicts, that define and shape national and local communities.

Smith, in describing her work in Los Angeles, reports that "the media became a very important character, so to speak, because the information that the media gave was really crucial. So they played this incredible role."[9] *Twilight* explores the archival impulse, or the drive toward premature closure and placement of a past event within a dominant narrative scheme, as enacted by the media sound bite, the public spokesperson, and the recorded image. In the case of the Rodney King incident, media texts such as news footage and video were central to Smith's examination of the event, its effect on the community, and its place within our cultural history. George Holliday's video of the Rodney King beating provided the public with a record, a visual statement of a traumatic event in which one man's body received dozens of blows that resulted in life-threatening injuries. The base reality that the video documents—that Rodney King was in fact beaten severely—remains uncontested. Rodney King's body suffered through a traumatic event. However, the meaning of the beating, the struggle to articulate his experience and its significance within a community, raises new questions about traumatic experience. These questions involve the actual events and the process of creating meaning from this reality, a process that can harm the communities or individuals represented within the historical narratives. For example, in *Twilight,* the monologue of Josie Morales—the Los Angeles city employee, neighbor to George Holliday, and direct witness to the King beating—focuses on her concerns about the trial. In spite of the fact that she saw the beating firsthand, Morales did not have the opportunity to testify at the trial because her testimony would have contradicted police officer Melanie Singer's version of the events. Morales describes the beating scene:

> I remember that they just not only hit him with sticks,
> they also kicked him,
> and one guy,
> one police officer, even pummeled his fist
> into his face,
> and they were kicking him.[10]

In the text version of the play, Morales's monologue immediately follows and responds to Charles Duke, who testified as the expert witness of the Los Angeles Police Department's use-of-force policies and practices. Duke's cold, quasi-scientific description of the weapons used against

King comes in contact with Morales's distress, as she recounts the savage and chaotic beating she immediately witnessed.

Through the Duke monologue, Smith undermines the defense strategy that included isolating the videotape images from historical context. Smith performs Duke's quasi-scientific stance, which loses its impermeability when he describes the political infighting surrounding the decisions about use-of-force techniques. Daryl Gates, it seems, resented that the city government would no longer allow the choke hold or upper-body-control hold because, as Duke explains,

> we had something like
> seventeen to twenty deaths in a period of about 1975–76 to 1982,
>   and
> they said it was associated with its being used on Blacks
> and Blacks were dying.[11]

Duke blames the increased use of PCP, the drug Rodney King was accused of being on, as justification for his beating. Hospital testing found no trace of the drug in his system. No mention is made of Gates's infamous comment that black neck anatomy requires an increased application of force for the hold to be effective. To Duke, the average police officer faces extreme risk and consequences because "Daryl Gates / and the Command staff were gonna do an 'in your face' to / the City / Council and the Police Commission."[12] Duke claims to have seen many cases in which people were beaten into submission, "some of them identical to Rodney King."[13] His monologue complicates and oftentimes contradicts his testimony at the criminal trial. As the expert witness, who interpreted each blow as falling within department policy, he failed to mention the internal conflicts surrounding the use-of-force techniques. The jurors' reading of Duke's testimony was based on a blanket acceptance of department policy as correct. The department, it would seem, was above politics in the jurors' eyes. As long as the officers acted in accordance with departmental policy, their behavior was beyond reproach. Duke's *Twilight* interview reveals the assumptions behind his own "expertise" and the jury's inability to question that authority. Smith's placement of these two monologues turns up the volume to allow Morales's voice, absent from the courtroom, to challenge the "expert" witness's exclusive claim to the voice-over interpretation of the silent video.

Through these competing interpretations of the videotaped violence, *Twilight* suggests the possibility of understanding the creation of histories within media-saturated contexts that rely on freeze-frame iconographies of race to deliver meaning rapidly.[14] The context within which a culture or its individuals interpret a crisis is of central concern both in Smith's performance and in relation to questions about art, traumatic experience, and witnessing. In an essay titled "'I'll See It When I Believe It': Rodney King and the Prison-House of Video," Frank P. Tomasulo points out the importance of understanding context and the levels of history in relation to the Los Angeles crisis:

> Frederic Jameson's observation that "history is what hurts" is literally true for both Rodney King and South Central Los Angeles. History hurt in the sheer facticity of the physical beating of one individual and in the material, social, and economic scars wrought on a minority community. King's bruises, the L.A. deaths, and the property damage were concrete and real cultural traumas, not a free play of signifiers—no matter how they were interpreted. But televisually mediated history also hurt, by creating a media morality play that transfixed U.S. viewers and fractured the American social fabric.[15]

Tomasulo describes a kind of secondary traumatization, one that occurs through the representation and interpretation of an event that in some way silences or distorts the experience of survivors. This analysis suggests Marianne Hirsch's *postmemory*, which involves processing traumatic experience through the repetition of representations of traumatic events connected to the individual through cultural or familial identification.[16] These representations do "not have the effect of desensitizing us to horror, or shielding us from shock, thus demanding an endless escalation of disturbing imagery." Instead, Hirsch argues, through these fixed representations, "compulsive and traumatic repetition connects the second generation to the first, *producing* rather than *screening* the effect of trauma that was lived so much more directly *as compulsive repetition* by survivors and contemporary witnesses." Hirsh claims, however, that artistic representations, by "displacing and recontextualizing these well-known images in their artistic work," counter the devastating effects of repetition, providing a "*mostly* helpful vehicle of working through a traumatic past."[17] Indeed, *Twilight* offers a way to encounter the representations of Los Angeles in crisis that disrupts the relentless, retraumatizing loop of the videotaped beating and the courtroom scene.[18]

In the courtroom, Rodney King never takes the witness stand. His absence, Houston Baker asserts in his essay "Scene . . . Not Heard," reflects a public reception of testimony from people of color that has created a rigid dichotomy between body and voice. Historically, bodies of color have entered the public space without voice and in body only. Their stories have been told by their displayed bodies, already marked as sexually and racially other within dominant cultural ideology. Again, Baker describes use of the voiceless body in testimonies of racial violence: "For the slave—even when he or she is a 'fugitive from southern violence'—is expected to remain silent. At northern abolitionist rallies, for example, the fugitive becomes the 'Negro exhibit.' She silently turns her back to the audience in order to display the stripes inflicted by the southern overseer's whip."[19] The scars are read as stories told through "silent display." The image of a damaged black body enters the public consciousness without a voice.

As *Twilight* uncovers, the "silent display" of Rodney King's body within public space has immediate and lasting consequences, suggesting that "visibility is a trap. . . . It summons surveillance and the law; it provokes voyeurism, fetishism, the colonialist/imperial appetite for possession."[20] Frantz Fanon's well-known words about the trap of visibility seem to echo in the courtroom. "I am overdetermined from without," Fanon writes in *Black Skin, White Masks*.[21] The testimony given in the criminal trial clearly defines Rodney King according to a racialized scheme in which his body must be read and reread as a threat to dominant values. Jurors and other spectators only have to recognize him as a black male to enact a plot that includes the erasure of his subjectivity. Instead of their hearing his voice or considering his suffering, King's body falls into what Fanon refers to as "a historico-racial schema," which relies on the perception of the black body to activate the myths and historically ingrained stereotypes buttressing racist ideology. Fanon describes this phenomenon: "The elements that I used had been provided for me not by 'residual sensations and perceptions primarily of a tactile, vestibular, kinesthetic, and visual character, but by the other, the white man, who had woven me out of a thousand details, anecdotes, stories. I thought what I had in hand was to construct a physiological self, to balance space, to localize sensations."[22] Within the conservative courtroom setting, the video functions as one of the "anecdotes" to which Fanon refers, reproducing the "historico-racial schema" and thwarting its potential as survivor testimony. There is no opportunity for King to claim his body within the setting of the courtroom. The "physiological self" of the video, the one writhing and wailing in pain, is replaced by a brute incapable of feeling human sensation. The transformation of King from human to monster exacerbates the traumatic impact of the video for an entire community, to whom the video serves as confirmation of a long-ignored reality.

Fanon desires to construct a new body to counter the iconic body that reproduces the trauma of history through the visual field and interactions in public space. His comparison between historico-racial and physiological bodies invokes the two different memory systems—explicit, or narrative, and implicit, or bodily memory—that Smith describes in her statement, "The body has a memory just as the mind does."[23] Like Fanon, instead of focusing on the culturally privileged visual or language-based memory, which also deploys with its cues the narratives of racial bias, Smith's performance searches for a memory found in bodily responses beyond the visual. To counteract the placement of the black male body into the "historico-racial schema" within the courtroom or the televisually mediated history that extends beyond the courtroom walls, one could look to Fanon's expression of the need "to construct a physiological self, to balance space, to localize sensations" as it operates within the performance of *Twilight: Los Angeles, 1992* and in Smith's work in general. In Smith's work, bodies of memory are constructed to give voice to the process of making meaning from traumatic moments. Smith offers her body as an intersection between private memory and public history, using her own body as an agent in the transmission of memory to provide this new public space. Instead of imposing a narrative from outside the individual, she searches for the place that language or visual rhetorics cannot contain, exposing the struggle with meaning that accompanies the traumatic experience.

In *Twilight*, Smith counters the trap of the visual with the voices of intimacy. When faced with the "acceleration of history," Nora explains, memory "has taken refuge in gestures and habits, in skills passed down by unspoken tradition, in the body's inherent self-knowledge, in unstudied reflexes and ingrained memories."[24] Smith searches, through her interview subjects, for what Nora refers to as the "intimacy of memory" to counter the "ephemeral film of current events" surrounding the trial and its aftermath. The search for this intimacy leads her to the body, and through her interviews, she allows the bodily memory a presence in public space by reproducing not only the words but also the gestures, affect, and body language of the interviewee. Smith's performance allows a space for bodily memory through what Shoshana Felman refers to as the "innovative figure of the witness," the "medium of testimony" whose empathy allows more than the "mere reporting of fact."[25] As Richard

Schechner has noted, Smith "absorbs the gestures, the tone of voice, the look, the intensity"[26] of her subjects, and in doing so, *Twilight* confronts the iconic body and the trap of visibility while articulating memory in its fragmented, contradictory, and intimately felt forms. After listening to hundreds of hours of interviews, Smith pieces together the monologues, "strategic[ally] highlighting, selecting samples and multiplying examples," choosing, however, in her compositions to challenge the power of what Nora refers to as our "intensely retinal and powerfully televisual memory"[27] and demonstrating memory's multiple sites of resonance: a scar or wound; a visceral reaction to reminders: restricted breathing, heart palpitations, and an overwhelming sense of dread; a memory embedded within another memory; absence or longing; and the terror in the face of a loved one.

For example, in the introduction to *Twilight* and through monologues such as Angela King's, the play exposes the limits of visibility when they describe the videotape of the King beating. When faced with the video image, many jurors could not hear King's cries: "Yet a juror in the federal civil trial told me that the rest of the jurors had difficulty hearing what she and King's aunt had heard. But when, during deliberations, they focused on the audio rather than the video image, their perspective changed. The physical image of Rodney King had to be taken away for them to agree he was in pain and responding to the beating."[28] The jurors' inability to acknowledge King's suffering reminds us of the library scene in *Sally's Rape*, the jailhouse scene in *Dessa Rose*, and the courtroom scene in *Venus*. The jurors could not see and hear King simultaneously because their reading of the visual testimony represented by his writhing body in the videotape contradicted the aural expression of physical pain, which demonstrates that a disembodied voice more convincingly conveys suffering within a racialized world. When reenacting Angela King's response to the scene of her nephew's suffering, Smith performs a similar function to the blind older woman in *Dessa Rose* who, with the intimacy of touch, "reads" Dessa's scars as testimony, although Nehemiah calls on her to find visual evidence to support his racist agenda to claim Dessa's body and discount her trauma. *Twilight* challenges the exclusive power of visibility by examining the body both as a site for cultural inscription within the dominant frame and as the locus of traumatic response.

Trauma scholars such as Cathy Caruth, Dori Laub, and Shoshana Felman have recognized the relationship between the intersubjective dynamic of witnessing and the survivor's struggle to make meaning from traumatic experience. Laub describes a level of witnessing that involves "being a witness to the process of witnessing itself."[29] This level of witnessing includes and reflects the two other types of witnessing, described by Laub as "the level of being a witness to oneself within experience" and "the level of being a witness to the testimonies of others."[30] These two levels involve a connection or the creation of a space in which the inner chaos of trauma transforms from a purely private, isolating encounter with the unspeakable into the public enactment of testimony. Two bodies must occupy or constitute this space, the survivor-witness and the listener-witness. Through their encounter they seek to find words, a common if fragmented language, to give voice to the silent images of traumatic memory. Although this relationship has been well examined, the complications that arise within traumatic response and witnessing encounters that cross identity differences, including race and gender, have not been adequately theorized; Smith's work begins at this underexplored point.

Moving beyond rigid binaries also involves exploring the point at which bodies are dis(re)membered, as incomplete constructions within cultural consciousness. Smith occupies the position of survivor and listener, emphasizing the process by which memory transforms from a purely private to a more externalized, public form. As Shoshana Felman posits, testimony is a speech act.[31] The body cannot be divorced from language, as the internal conflict is externalized and made meaningful through the encounter between two bodies. Smith describes in her autobiography, *Talk to Me*, her fascination with language as enacting identity: "I believe identity is a process and that we are [at this] very moment making an adjustment, and sometimes those moments happen when we're talking."[32] Indeed, Smith's technique and structure are concerned with the process through which the individual's identity shifts and forms in relation to the transmission of memory. And the expression and reception—the transaction of meaning—become as important as the words themselves. The work recalls Karen Malpede's assertions: "Because theatre takes place in public and involves the movement of bodies across a stage, theatre seems uniquely suited to portray the complex interpersonal realities of trauma and to give shape to the compelling interventions that become possible when trauma is addressed by others who validate the victims' reality."[33] Through Smith's performance, we can see that the survivor struggles to define his or her experience, enacting the "complex interpersonal realities of trauma." The performance also points to the internal obstacles caused by trauma and the external conflict with the dominant ideology that may be complicit in the initial trauma and in silencing the survivor's voice.

According to Bessel van der Kolk, "since the early part of [the twentieth] century very few published systematic studies have used patients' own reports to explore the nature of traumatic memories."[34] Perhaps the reason for this neglect is that the survivor speaks in the broken language described by Smith. Rather than the closed narrative of fact pursued in the courtroom, survivor testimony "does not offer . . . a completed statement, a totalizable account of those events."[35] Smith's performance of *Twilight: Los Angeles, 1992* problematizes the master narratives of the courtroom and mainstream media and builds new narratives from the broken speech of the crisis. Smith inserts another body of evidence, her own, at the scene to destabilize the absolute authority of the visual and challenge the quest for fact.

When interviewing individuals involved in the crisis, Smith searches for the residue of trauma found in the body language and speech patterns of subjects and intentionally seeks the moments when the individuals "lose their grammar."[36] "In L.A.," Smith explains, "people were less articulate, which was a good thing for me because I'm looking for the place where language fails, where people have to struggle to find words."[37] We see, for example, an agitated Ruben Martinez, a journalist who has witnessed the police abuse of the Los Angeles Latino community, who tells Smith in a clearly pained, outraged voice, "Even if you're doing all the right things . . . it's . . . you're—you're—you're—you're . . . there's still something *wrong* with you."[38] Smith's pursuit of the break in language supports Shoshana Felman's suggestion that "as a relation to events, testimony seems to be composed of bits and pieces of a memory that has been overwhelmed by occurrences that have not settled into understanding or remembrance, acts that cannot be constructed as knowledge nor assimilated into full cognition, events in excess of our frame of reference."[39] Those moments for which Smith searches, the breaking points of language, are portals of entry into a forgotten world. They reveal the bodies buried in memory, left outside history, what Sander Gilman refers to as "the half-remembered bodies of the past."[40] In *Twilight*, the voices break away from the initial question posed and move as if guided by another force.

In Smith's search for a place that language will not hold, her performance fragments the dominant narrative, reveals the painful condition of fragmentation within traumatized communities, and rebuilds a new community in the aesthetic space of her performance. Julia Salverson posits that "acts of witnessing may be possible through a theatre that sets out to pose questions and not to provide answers."[41] In an interview with Smith, Carol Martin characterizes Smith's apparent commitment to documenting an event without allowing its multiplicity to congeal into a single, absolute form: "Instead of trying to make a cohesive picture," Martin tells Smith, "you revealed different landscapes of emotions and histories."[42] Or as Sandra Richards puts it, "Smith's artistry unsettles as it delights: it challenges viewers to locate—and relocate—themselves within a kaleidoscope of oftentimes contradictory positions. It presumes and speaks to a desire for community even while dramatizing the fractured quality of contemporary social networks."[43] The lack of cohesion comes from Smith's resistance to constructing a seamless narrative from the many stories she receives in her interviews. In both form and content, Smith's text and performance signify the friction, inconsistency, and fragmentation that exist in the "real" world of her characters and audiences. The fragments with jagged edges bleed into the space around them instead of becoming polished, fabricated bits of packaged information. Fragments in memory and in language suggest an effort reorganize the world in relation to a traumatic experience. The stutters, shifts, and meanderings that characterize Smith's compositions offer insight into the struggle to understand and to articulate an identity in relation to the catastrophic events in Los Angeles. The dislocations and disruptions in the interviewed subjects' speech interrupt the self-conscious narratives they construct to position and define themselves in relation to the crisis, revealing the points at which the narratives they construct contain their own undoing; the narratives can never contain the truth of the crisis.

By emphasizing these fractured moments, *Twilight* questions narratives that close off alternative meanings. Dorinne Kondo argues that Smith's experimental structure does not provide a single protagonist with whom the audience can identify; instead all voices share the stage. Kondo continues, "By inviting spectators into identification and then problematizing that identification, Smith's cross-racial and cross-gender representation problematizes notions of stable subject-positions, highlighting instead the forging of those positions in the matrices of power."[44] Through this decentered structure, the play does not, however, promote instability or exalt the fragment. Fragmentation does not end, but neither does the desire for and drive toward cohesion, which creates testimony that "captures the specificity of the cultural sources of fragmentation and the effect on an individual psyche"[45] and explores the way in which "fragmentation arises historically, from private and public developmental traumas."[46] *Twilight* enacts, as Homi Bhabha explains, the political responsibility of individuals working in the realm of cultural criticism to "attempt to fully realize, and take responsibility for, the unspoken, unrepresented pasts that haunt the historical present."[47] The "unspoken" to which Bhabha refers involves the traumatic legacy of racism that remains unaccounted for within the "acceleration of history," even as current iterations reactivate responses deeply embedded within our psyches. Therefore, although it may be productive to contest the seamlessness of historical narrative, specifically as it supports and reproduces dominant ideologies of racism and sexism, it would be ineffective and disempowering to reject completely the desire for cohesion in the stories constructed by subaltern communities whose collective memories and cultural identity have been denied by cultural imperialism.

Communities are made and unmade in *Twilight* as obvious alignments shift and new connections emerge. Kai Erikson's assertion that "trauma has both centripetal and centrifugal tendencies. It draws one away from the center of group space while at the same time drawing one back."[48] Ricardo Ainslie and Kalina Brabeck confirm Erickson's assertion when discussing communities in crisis:

> collective responses to trauma often lend themselves to powerful, fragmentation-prone impulses, what we term *centrifugal tendencies*. They do so, in part, because traumatizing incidents typically activate a broader collective memory of traumatization . . . link[ing] the present traumatic incident to prior incidents suffered by the group or community, and the emotions that are part of those past grievances and injustices become fused with the present circumstances in ways that can be quite destructive when the *centrifugal processes* gain ascendancy.[49]

Twilight negotiates the difficulty in mapping out or defining community in the constantly shifting ground of the post-traumatic period. These shifts occur in relation to the community's experience of its own history flooding the boundaries of its present. "In trauma we are untimely ripped," writes Juliet Mitchell,[50] referring to the past-presence created within the individual's psyche in traumatic experience. Trauma obliterates organizing schemes, and as Mitchell goes on to explain, "Psychoanalysis is equipped to contribute to the understanding of the reaction to trauma, not to the trauma itself." Mitchell captures the belatedness of trauma; traumatic experience only exists in memory because it exceeds the individual's capacity to exist within the event, except in a state of shock or nonbeing.[51]

This "nonbeing," this alienation from one's material present and bodily presence, is dramatized in the section of *Twilight* titled "War Zone," which ends with the words of Dean Gilmour, an official at the Los Angeles County coroner's office. Part of the "clean-up crew," Gilmour tries to offer statistics for the dead, including sex, ethnicity, and cause of death. He stresses, however, that the facts cannot be confirmed. His office is still in the process of investigating each incident. He begins by referring to one family whose daughter has been missing since April, presumably killed in a store fire. Her body has never been found, even though the site has been searched multiple times for physical traces, or "human remains." The absence of her body has caused the family tremendous pain: "The family doesn't have . . . / They can't really get on with their life until they have / some / resolution to it."[52] This final piece in the "War Zone" section refuses to provide closure as well. In the shocking aftermath of traumatic experience, the body is both always present and absent, nowhere and everywhere. Attempts to locate the body are thwarted, and it remains outside the official record of the event. Instead of being accounted for in statistics, the body can only be measured in loss and unfulfilled desire for closure for loved ones.

The body in the Gilmour monologue remains outside any community; neither the family nor society can identify or claim it. This loss relates to the fundamental shattering of identity that occurs with traumatic experience. "Trauma," Juliet Mitchell writes, "can reactivate aspects of autistic states in anyone because some degree of rejection of the body, some sense of the body as alien, is probably the human lot."[53] Unable to communicate experience, remaining closed off and alienated, the survivor's story remains trapped within a body that now seems strange and unknown as well. "The core experiences of psychological trauma," according to Judith Herman, "are disempowerment and disconnection from others. Recovery, therefore, is based upon the empowerment of the survivor and the creation of new connections. Recovery can take place only within the context of relationships; it cannot occur in isolation."[54] Smith pieces together a whole from the interviews, reintegrating individual voices that have been isolated in trauma into a community of survivors.

The recovery or identification of bodies does not occur in isolation but requires a community effort, as the Gilmour piece implies. Questions about identity, trauma, and the body emerge in the process of fleshing out the memory in *Twilight*.[55] Smith constructs monologues from her interviews with African American, Chicano, Latino, and Korean American survivors of the riots that include an emphasis on bodily injury and unhealed psychic wounds. Brutalized bodies figure prominently in *Twilight*, but in contrast to the trial scene, these images correspond directly to the intimacy of memory of those individuals directly involved. Although the trial did not include the testimony of Rodney King but only the visual image of his beating, *Twilight* connects the perception of the visual record with receiving the oral testimony of survivors. For example, Michael Zinzun, a community activist who won a police-brutality lawsuit, lost sight in one of his eyes after a police beating. In his office, he keeps graphic photographs of bodies bloodied and battered by the Los Angeles Police Department, including one of "a man with part of his skull blown off and part of his body in the chest area blown off, so you can see his organs."[56] This scene powerfully counteracts the one in the courtroom when the defense uses the visual evidence of Rodney King's brutalization against him. In the first line of Zinzun's monologue, he tells Smith, "I have witnessed police abuse," countering the efforts to read this violence in relation to any use-of-force policy. Instead of sealing trauma's radical disconnect, the sense of alienation from one's own body-in-experience, in a seamless narrative, the monologue exposes the unmanageable loss and the always incomplete efforts to communicate this loss.

Several monologues serve to piece together the personal and cultural legacy of brutalized bodies within the Los Angeles community. Rudy Salas, the Chicano artist who opens the text version of the play, describes his fractured ear drum after a police beating,[57] following his own traumatic history with an account of his son's encounter with the police. Salas asks the painful question, "How do you think a father feels, stuff that happened to me fifty years ago happened to my son?"[58] A shared history, one not accounted for within the pages of the "official" history, binds Salas's experience with his son and other members of his community. Salas describes the beating he survived, which resulted in a loss of hearing. In another moment, Julio Mnejivar recounts his experience during the riots, which included watching his mother, sister, and grandmother almost shot by national guard troops, witnessing a man being slapped for speaking Spanish, and seeing another man crying because the handcuffs were too tight.[59] Theresa Allison, founder of Mothers Reclaiming Our Children (Mothers ROC), offers the story of her nephew's shooting by police, an event that shattered her family:

My son changed.
(*She's crying*)
Other guys in Watts changed.
Our life totally changed
from happy people
to hurting people.
I mean hurting people,
I mean *hurting,*
pain.[60]

While talking about her nephew Tiny, who died after a policewoman shot him in the face, Theresa Allison describes this same officer's routine violence against African American youth:

she used to go in an' pull these kids,
I mean from twelve years old,
and kick 'em and hit their heads against trees
and stomp on the ground.
Why you got to do Black kids like that?[61]

These intimate voices form a dynamic testimony to trauma's resonance within the bodies of the living, showing how each new blow conjures up old wounds that threaten to overwhelm the subject once again.

Angela King's monologue illustrates this phenomenon compellingly. Rodney's aunt begins with a seemingly unrelated comparison between her life and the Dorothy Dandridge film *Carmen.* The comparison leads to a story about her mother stabbing her father and subsequently serving a prison sentence that left the children without parents. "My brother and I were the only two that stayed together," she explains, "and that brother was the father of Rodney."[62] Throughout her discussion, she refers back to Rodney's father. It becomes clear that the beating evokes the pain of that earlier trauma for her and in many ways violates her place of safety in memory, the one connection she managed to preserve after the devastating loss of her parents, her relationship with her brother. In her comparison, neither the film *Carmen* nor the videotaped beating replace or shape memory; rather, they evoke the texture of memory: the sights, sounds, and emotions of previous relationships and experiences.

By composing monologues that counter the immediacy of the visual field, *Twilight* shifts the focus from the scene or seen to the act of seeing, from an objectifying gaze toward the subjectivity of perception. In this way, the process of creating meaning from the actual reality of an event in history can then be seen in relation to the multiple perspectives. *Twilight* seeks an answer to Wendy Chun's questions, "How then can we negotiate multiple and possibly conflicting testimonies between witnesses? . . . How, then, can we listen and respond to testimony so that one testimony does not substitute for another, but rather resonates with it?"[63] Answering these questions requires an examination of the ways in which post-traumatic response and its retreat into rigid, "black and white" reaction can deepen the grooves of an already well-worn recording in race relations. As an African American woman portraying characters across racial, gender, ethnic, age, and class lines, Smith reveals through her performance the complex negotiation of identity formation in a multiethnic community, affirming Peggy Phelan's assertion that "identity is perceptible only through a relation to an other—which is to say, it is a form of both resisting and claiming the other, declaring the boundary where the self diverges from and merges with the other."[64] The collective and individual identities find meaning only in relation to each other. *Twilight* uses the opportunity that the crisis provides, with its instability and gray, mutable moments, to reveal the narrative processing around the event as it reiterates racial or ethnic identity. Both the formation of racial identities and the act of witnessing require an intersubjective dynamic, but they work at cross purposes. In white supremacy, the relationship between black and white allows white to form as a superior identity at the expense of the black subject. In the witnessing relationship, one needs to move from the isolation of traumatic experience into a symbolic, meaning-making encounter, and the witness needs to suspend his or her own ego boundaries to accept the burden of the trauma. It is precisely the struggle between these two types of dynamics that *Twilight* negotiates when attempting to reconnect the multiple forms of memory fragmented through crisis.

As Frank H. Wu points out, "Race relations, like bad relationships of any type, can become fixed and unchanging. Parties use accusatory absolutes. 'Never' and 'always' rule out a range of options and prevent mutual and free exchanges of information and ideas. One side becomes the villain, the other the victim. As crude caricatures, both give up free will and neither can claim moral responsibility."[65] Smith's monologues bring to the fore the issues around visibility, race, and traumatic experience, resisting a reliance on one type of representation or one type of memory based in the visual field. Neither the community nor the event becomes simplified or essentialized, or as Dorinne Kondo observes, "In a deft double movement, Smith de-essentializes race while holding on to the awareness that race remains a powerful social force that requires social critique and shapes the reception of her work."[66] Through this innovative process, Smith proposes the possibility of an intersubjective witnessing dynamic that challenges the rigid schemas of race and unaddressed traumatic response.

Twilight moves beyond a frame that defines race relations in the United States only in terms of a black-and-white racial binary. Moving beyond black and white also confronts post-traumatic response at its core. Although trauma causes a breakdown in organizing schemes and the symbolic order, the post-traumatic experience is characterized by rigid, inflexible, binary or "black and white" thinking. In "The Black/White Binary Paradigm of Race," Juan F. Perea argues that "the paradigm dictates that all other racial identities and groups in the United States are best understood through the Black/White binary paradigm. Only a few writers even recognize that they use a Black/White paradigm as a frame of reference through which to understand all racial relations."[67] Smith attempts to move beyond this paradigm in her selection of interview subjects, and she refers in the play's introduction to dramaturgs Dorinne Kondo and Hector Tobar, who "passionately attacked the black-and-white canvas that most of us in the room were inclined to perpetuate"[68] and who helped shape the production toward the inclusion of Chicano, Latino, and Korean American perspectives.

In "Traces of the Master Narrative in the Story of African American/Korean American Conflict: How We Constructed 'Los Angeles,'" Lisa C. Ikemoto argues that it is "white supremacy's prescriptive, conflict-constructing power, which deploys exclusionary concepts of race and privilege in ways that maintain intergroup conflict." She elaborates, "Further interrogation suggests that despite the absence of obvious whiteness in a conflict described as intergroup, culturally embedded white supremacy (racism) provides the operative dynamic."[69] Young-Soon Han and the Park family provide insight into feelings of disconnection and disillusionment caused by a failed American dream. In June Park's home, which Smith notes is "an imitation of the European aesthetic,"[70] Park tries to make sense of what happened to her husband, Walter, who had a partial lobotomy after a gunshot wound in the head. June Park struggles to understand her husband's fate after he adhered so closely to the rules of the American dream:

[he] donated a lot of money to the Compton area.
And he knows the City Council,
the policemen, they knows him.
Then why,
why he has to get shot?[71]

In a section of *Twilight* titled "Swallowing the Bitterness," Young-Soon Han wonders, "why do we have to be left out?"[72] With palpable anger and grief, she describes watching televised news coverage of the African American response to the civil trial, revealing that she believes her voice remains unheard. In this moment, Young-Soon Han identifies with the joy expressed by the televised representatives of the Los Angeles African American community but also describes her bitterness, a "fire" within her that speaks to the unresolved conflict continuing to smolder as long as her suffering goes unacknowledged. Frank H. Wu writes that "it was white police officers who had flagrantly violated the civil rights of King, but it was Asian Americans who paid the price. It was not exclusively African American and Latino young men who made up the roving mobs that went on a criminal rampage, but it was Asian Americans who were besieged."[73] The perspective represented in Wu's analysis does not appear in most mainstream interpretations of the events, but it is evoked in the traumatic legacy suggested by Young-Soon Han and the Parks.

Twilight allows for the testimony of Los Angeles communities without eliding the differences or critical disparities, especially the material ones. *Twilight* offers a public space in which to bear witness to the complexities of the riots, which Lisa Lowe argues

> are the most vivid eruption of the contradiction between multicul-
> turalism as the representation of the liberal state and the material
> poverty and disenfranchisement that are the conditions of those
> represented. Though the U.S. media consistently attempted to con-
> struct the crisis as a racial conflict between Blacks and Koreans, the
> looters enraged by the King verdict were not only Blacks but also
> Chicanos, Latinos, and working-class whites; all violently objected
> to the denial of brutally racialized economic stratification.[74]

In *Twilight*, the "economic stratification" is brought into full view as every monologue occurs within a material context, such as a living room or an office, that cannot be divorced from the testimony. In this way, Smith's play creates what Nora refers to as sites of memory that counter the acceleration of history, or media-ated "narratives that suppress tension and opposition [to] suggest we have already achieved multiculturalism" and that "allow us to ignore the profound and urgent gaps, the inequalities and conflicts, among racial, ethnic, and immigrant groups."[75] As Nora puts it, "There are *lieux de memoire*, sites of memory, because there are no longer *milieux de memoire*, real environments of memory."[76]

Within *Twilight*, two subjects reveal the desire for a public memory or alternative spaces for re-membering the bodies of the Los Angeles crisis. These sites of memory would forge cross-cultural connections in unexpected, unsettling spaces and attempt to control the visual representation and reception of the riots. They provide insight into the survivor's need to resist hegemonic control of the representation and reception of the event. Reginald Denny describes a room in which he hopes to display the letters of support he received after his beating. He tells Smith, "It'll just be a fun thing to be in there,/just like a fun thing,/there won't be a color problem/in this room."[77] Another subject acts as a response in many ways to Denny's desire to create a space of unity. Paul Parker begins his testimony by referring to the L.A. Four, the defendants in the Reginald Denny beating. He wants to have "just one room/set aside. It's going to be my No Justice No Peace Room."[78] His explanation of the concept behind his room is filled with pauses, captured in the text by ellipses and "um":

> you know, with No Justice No Peace
> it's . . . its,
> you know, um,
> I guess you might say it's fairly simple,
> but to me it's pretty, um,
> not complex,
> but then again it's deep,
> it's nothing shallow.[79]

Parker's struggle for definition reflects the complicated process of creating a space to bear witness to the crisis, a space in which language does not fix meaning. The Denny and Parker monologues both reveal the desire to counteract the "acceleration of history," which would leave the event in the distant past, with stories forgotten or untold and traumatic experience unarticulated by those individuals who lived through the crisis of 1992.

The legal scholar and critical race theorist Mari Matsuda has suggested that "linguistic anxiety is the new proxy for racial anxiety."[80] "What history has given us," Matsuda contends, "is speech—linguistic space—as a playing ground on which we struggle for power and ascendancy."[81]

A crisis such as the one in Los Angeles provides an opportunity in this struggle for new definitions and alternative histories to enter public consciousness, or at least to enact Lydia Liu's desire to "rethink the nation as a territory of struggle between competing subject positions, narratives, and voices where nationalism or nationalisms may win, as they have indeed won in many parts of the world, but cannot wipe out the traces of the struggle."[82] The struggle over linguistic space and the representation of a traumatic cultural past produces what Antonius C. G. M. Robben refers to as a "contestive relation" in cultural memory, "which keeps [opposing cultural groups] hostage to each other's memory politics. . . . People cannot mourn their losses when others deny that those losses took place."[83] This struggle and its resulting anxiety indeed function as a substitute for racial conflict at that particular moment in Los Angeles. *Twilight* illuminates the competing forces attempting to define the significance of the crisis within the national history or to determine how story becomes incorporated into the national framework. Smith refers to this struggle to define racial issues: "I think there's an assumption that the public want to know what the spokespeople are saying. But we can't depend on the spokespeople to define race anymore. That definition is ultimately going to have to come from the community."[84] "It is a critical question," Bessel van der Kolk explains, "whether public acknowledgment and validation of the personal suffering of traumatized individuals in places such as Rwanda, Bosnia, Lebanon, Cambodia, and the inner cities of the United States is a useful social process that can promote a shared sense of trust, empathy and personal responsibility. Can individuals and nations afford to face the awful truths about their past, as long as life's basic necessities have not been provided for?"[85] When the state offers no opportunity for justice and renders meaningless the history of oppression that traumatizes communities, art can provide a public space in which bodies and memories unite to offer testimony. The challenge defined by van der Kolk, to create public contexts that acknowledge the suffering of individuals and communities, is in many ways undertaken by Anna Deavere Smith in *Twilight: Los Angeles, 1992. Twilight* explores the possibility of recognizing bodies of memory beyond the scene of history.

* * *

Traumatic Possessions concludes with Smith's gesture toward incorporating the testimony of contemporary trauma survivors within a larger context that accounts for the residue of past trauma in families and communities. To return to Nicholas Abraham's work on transgenerational traumatic haunting, "Reducing the 'phantom' entails reducing the sin attached to someone else's secret and stating it in acceptable terms so as to defy, circumvent, or domesticate the phantom's (and our) resistances."[86] Secrets acquire the weight of sin when survivors remain silenced in shame by perpetrators or when cultural forces deem their voices unworthy of witness. This sin accretes in and through the body and its encounters. By returning to the body, which Smith performs with all its accumulated knowledge and its complex relations to place, identity, memory, and other bodies, Smith reduces the phantom, the painful but unspoken legacy of unresolved collective and familial trauma. Smith's characters join Ursa Corregidora in the search for understanding the consequences of past violence on their current lives, only unlike Ursa, they raise their voices surrounded by other perspectives also affected immediately by the events of 1991–92. Performed by a black female subject in a racially charged public space, these perspectives include implicitly Venus, Ursa, Dessa, and Sally and their compromised efforts to bear witness to suffering in their historical moment. And at last the body once possessed by a traumatic legacy voices its truth.

Notes

Introduction

1. Felman and Laub, *Testimony*, 59.
2. Ibid., 57.
3. Ibid., 68.
4. Ibid., 58.
5. Schaffer and Smith, "Conjunctions," 9.
6. Douglass and Vogler, *Witness and Memory*, 25.
7. Schaffer and Smith, "Conjunctions," 9–10.
8. See, for example, Carl Gutierrez-Jones's *Critical Race Narratives,* Claudia Tate's *Psychoanalysis and Black Novel,* and the special issue on "Postcolonial Trauma Novels" in *Studies in the Novel* 40, nos. 1–2 (Spring–Summer 2008).
9. Zwarg, "Du Bois on Trauma," 1–2.
10. For an extended analysis of Freud's abandonment of his seduction theory, see Masson's *The Assault on Truth.*
11. Zwarg, "Du Bois on Trauma," 1–2.
12. Brooks Bouson, *Quiet as It's Kept,* 7.
13. Spillers, "All the Things You Could Be by Now," 138.
14. Ibid., 136.
15. Eyerman, *Cultural Trauma,* 3.
16. Kirmayer, "Landscapes of Memory," 175.
17. Sharpley-Whiting, *Black Venus,* 10.
18. Fanon, *Black Skin, White Masks,* 113–14.
19. Bakare-Yusuf, "Economy of Violence," 316.
20. Baker, "Scene . . . Not Heard," 40.
21. Smith, *Twilight,* xx.
22. Scarry, *The Body in Pain,* 13.
23. LaCapra, *Writing History, Writing Trauma,* 78.

24. Scarry, *The Body in Pain,* 14.

25. King, *African Americans and the Culture of Pain*, 8.

26. Ibid., 17.

27. Ibid.

28. Popular examinations of black pain include Kristal Brent Zook's *Black Women's Lives* and Charlotte Pierce-Baker's *Surviving Silence: Black Women's Stories of Rape.* These texts offer perspectives on black women's lives that do not shy away from difficult material, and they convey an understanding of the traumatic experiences of contemporary black women that incorporates racism's insidious effects. Pierce-Baker's volume begins with an epigraph from *Corregidora* about the memory coming alive through language, suggesting the merging of memory forms in testimony.

29. Taussig, *The Nervous System*, 49.

30. Butler, "Endangered/Endangering," 16.

31. Louis, "Body Language," 141.

32. Ibid., 143, 146.

33. De Certeau, *The Practices of Everyday Life*, 108.

34. Abraham and Torok, *The Shell and the Kernel*, 189.

1 / "The Quick Gasp of Sympathy"

1. Williams, *Dessa Rose*, 10.

2. Rushdy, *Neoslave Narratives* , 3–4.

3. Williams, *Dessa Rose*, 56–57.

4. Henderson, "Speaking in Tongues," 126–27.

5. Mercer, "Dialogue," 137.

6. Felman and Laub, *Testimony*, 67.

7. Williams, *Dessa Rose*, 58.

8. Herman, *Trauma and Recovery*, 133–214.

9. Frankenberg, "When We Are Capable of Stopping, We Begin to See," 4.

10. Friedman, "Beyond White and Other," 17.

11. Morrison, *Playing the Dark*, 12.

12. Kirmayer, "Landscapes of Memory," 182.

13. Williams, *Dessa Rose*, , 51.

14. Ibid., 4.

15. Ibid., 13.

16. Culbertson, "Embodied Memory," 169.

17. Williams, *Dessa Rose*, 10.

18. Felman and Laub, *Testimony*, 17.

19. Williams, *Dessa Rose*, 16.

20. Williams, *Give Birth to Brightness*, 218.

21. Hammonds, "Toward a Genealogy of Black Female Sexuality," 170.

22. Williams, *Dessa Rose*, 57.

23. Ibid., 90.

24. Ibid.

25. Ibid., 105.

26. Sanchez, "The Estrangement Effect," 23.

27. Ibid., 144.

28. Ibid., 145.

29. Ibid., 166–67.
30. Ibid., 171.
31. Ibid., 170.
32. Ibid., 198.
33. Ibid., 199.
34. Ibid., 207.
35. Griffin, "Textual Healing," 531.
36. Williams, *Dessa Rose*, 220.
37. hooks, "Representing Whiteness in the Black Imagination," 341.
38. Caruth, *Unclaimed Experience*, 133.
39. Griffin, "Textual Healing," 521.
40. Williams, *Dessa Rose*, 260.
41. For an examination of this historical event in relation to the Parks play, see Sara L. Warner's "Suzan-Lori Parks's Drama of Disinternment."

2 / Betrayal Trauma and the Test of Complicity in Suzan-Lori Parks's *Venus*

1. "Look beneath the Surface."
2. Demleitner, "The Law at a Crossroads," 259.
3. Ibid.
4. J. Smith, "Why British Men Are Rapists," 15.
5. Altrick, *The Shows of London*, 270.
6. Parks borrows this line from a broadsheet ballad that begins, "The storie of the Hottentot ladie and her lawful knight," reprinted in Hayward and Leader's *Romantic Period Writings, 1798–1832*, 101. Parks, *Venus*, 72.
7. Parks, *Venus*, 69.
8. Miller, "The Bottom of Desire," 135.
9. Elam and Rayner, "Body Parts," 277.
10. Marneweck, "Staging Stereotype and Performing the Exotic Erotic," 56.
11. Parks, *Venus*, 62.
12. Ibid., 63.
13. Ibid., 75.
14. Ibid., 76.
15. Ibid.
16. Elam and Rayner, "Body Parts," 267.
17. J. Young, "The Re-objectification and Re-commodification of Saartjie Baartman," 699.
18. Ibid., 699–700.
19. Quoted in ibid., 700.
20. LaCapra, *Writing History*, 15.
21. Ibid., 4.
22. H. Young, "Touching History," 144.
23. Parks, *Venus*, 15.
24. Ibid., 19.
25. Ibid., 83–84.
26. Ibid., 46.
27. Ibid., 51.
28. Herman, *Trauma and Recovery*, 75.

29. Parks, *Venus,* 56–57.
30. Freyd, *Betrayal Trauma,* 129.
31. Schiebinger, *Nature's Body,* 168–72.
32. Sharpley-Whiting, *Black Venus,* 24–25.
33. Freyd, *Betrayal Trauma,* 165.
34. Parks, *Venus,* 135.
35. Ibid., 144.
36. Ibid., 118.
37. Ibid., 91.
38. Scarry, *The Body in Pain,* 34.
39. Lifton, *Nazi Doctors,* 16.
40. Fausto-Sterling, "Gender, Race, and Nation," 22.
41. Parks, *Venus,* 26.
42. Ibid., 156.
43. Herman, *Trauma and Recovery,* 75.

3 / Between Women

1. McCauley, *Sally's Rape,* 225.
2. McCauley, "Thoughts on My Career," 269.
3. Nymann, "*Sally's Rape*: Robbie McCauley's Survival Art," 577.
4. Schneider, *The Explicit Body in Performance,* 174–75.
5. Ibid., 2.
6. Caruth and Keenan, "The AIDS Crisis Is Not Over," 258.
7. Ibid.
8. Robben, "How Traumatized Societies Remember," 127.
9. Ibid.
10. Caruth and Keenan, "The AIDS Crisis Is Not Over," 258.
11. Harris, "Failing 'White Woman,'" 186–87.
12. Hammonds, "Toward a Genealogy of Black Female Sexuality," 170.
13. Roach, *Cities of the Dead,* 25–26.
14. Fanon, *Black Skin, White Masks,* 111.
15. Ibid., 112.
16. Ibid., 111.
17. Foucault, *Language, Counter-Memory, Practice,* 148.
18. Ibid.
19. Fanon, *Black Skin, White Masks,* 111.
20. Roach, *Cities of the Dead,* 25.
21. Dolan, *The Feminist Spectator as Critic,* 107.
22. McCauley, *Sally's Rape,* 222.
23. Patraka, "Robbie McCauley," 206.
24. Malpede, "Teaching Witnessing," 168–69.
25. Ibid.,168.
26. Ibid.
27. Felman and Laub, *Testimony,* 75.
28. Quoted in Rosenfeld, "Spectators at Stage Center."
29. Harris, "Failing 'White Woman,'" 184.
30. McCauley, *Sally's Rape,* 225.

31. Ibid., 228.

32. Ibid., 233.

33. McCauley, "Thoughts on My Career," 275.

34. Ibid.

35. Thompson, "Blackface, Rape, and Beyond," 124.

36. Patraka, "Robbie McCauley," 215.

37. McCauley, *Sally's Rape*, 222.

38. Patraka, "Robbie McCauley," 212.

39. McCauley, *Sally's Rape*, 231.

40. Bakare-Yusuf, "The Economy of Violence," 316.

41. McKay, "Alice Walker's 'Advancing Luna—and Ida B. Wells,'" 249.

42. Brownmiller, *Against Our Will*, 216.

43. Ibid., 279.

44. Davis, *Woman, Race, and Class*, 73.

45. Ibid., 182.

46. V. Smith, "Split Affinities," 273.

47. hooks, "Feminism as a Persistent Critique of History," 78.

48. McCauley, *Sally's Rape*, 228.

49. Williams, *Give Birth to Brightness*, 218.

50. Patraka, "Robbie McCauley," 207.

51. McCauley addresses this issue in her interview in *Conjure Women*.

52. McCauley, *Sally's Rape*, 228.

53. Christensen, "With Whom Do You Believe Your Lot Is Cast?'" 619.

54. McCauley, *Sally's Rape*, 235.

55. Frankenberg, *White Women, Race Matters*, 240.

56. McCauley, "Thoughts on My Career," 275.

57. McCauley, *Sally's Rape*, 226.

58. Patraka, "Robbie McCauley," 216.

59. McCauley, *Sally's Rape*, 232.

60. Ibid.

61. Patraka, "Robbie McCauley," 216.

62. Forte, "Focus on the Body," 251.

63. McCauley, *Sally's Rape*, 231.

64. Patraka, "Robbie McCauley," 207.

65. McCauley, *Conjure Women*, 216.

66. Ibid., 206.

67. Ibid., 214.

68. Ibid., 216.

69. Diamond, *Unmaking Mimesis*, 168.

70. McCauley, *Sally's Rape*, 228.

71. Bakare-Yusuf, "The Economy of Violence," 314. Caruth, *Trauma: Explorations in Memory*, 4.

72. de Certeau, *The Practices of Everyday Life*, 108.

73. Root, "Reconstructing the Impact of Trauma on Personality," 373.

74. "The Rape of Black Women as a Weapon of Terror" is the title to an entire section, beginning on page 173, within Lerner's documentary history *Black Women in White America*.

75. Patraka, "Robbie McCauley," 213–14.

76. Salverson, "Performing Emergency," 183.

4 / Uncanny Spaces

1. Felman and Laub, *Testimony*, 65.

2. Trinh T. Minh-ha, *Woman, Native, Other*, 122. Gilbert and Gubar, *The Madwoman in the Attic*, 49.

3. McFarlane and van der Kolk, "Trauma and Its Challenge to Society," 27.

4. Morgenstern, "Mother's Milk and Sister's Blood," 105.

5. LaCapra, *Writing History, Writing Trauma*, 186.

6. Caruth, *Unclaimed Experience*, 61.

7. Nadar, "Violence," 581.

8. Root, "Reconstructing the Impact of Trauma on Personality," 241.

9. Kirmayer, "Landscapes of Memory," 75.

10. Abraham, "Notes on the Phantom," 289.

11. Ibid., 287.

12. Rubin, "Thinking Sex," 4.

13. Goldberg, "Living the Legacy," 451. See also Elizabeth Yukins's "Bastard Daughters and the Possession of History in *Corregidora* and *Paradise*."

14. Jones, *Corregidora*, 127.

15. Ibid., 128.

16. Brown, "Not Outside the Range," 102.

17. Jones, *Corregidora*, 125.

18. Freud, "The Uncanny," 220.

19. Bronfen, *Over Her Dead Body*, 113.

20. Bronfen, "From Omphalos to Phallus," 151.

21. Freud, "The Uncanny," 224.

22. Felman and Laub, *Testimony*, 63.

23. Bartky, "The Pedagogy of Shame," 225.

24. Ibid., 225.

25. Jones, *Corregidora*, 42, 45.

26. Ibid., 151.

27. Ibid., 46.

28. Ibid., 45.

29. Ibid., 77.

30. Anzaldúa, *Borderlands/La Frontera*, 48; Root, "Reconstructing the Impact of Trauma on Personality," 104.

31. Anzaldúa, *Borderlands/La Frontera*, 73.

32. Ibid., 48.

33. Caruth, "An Interview with Robert Jay Lifton," 137–38.

34. Kirmayer, "Landscapes of Memory," 175.

35. Freud, "Uncanny," 245.

36. Jones, *Corregidora*, 11.

37. Felman and Laub, *Testimony*, 17.

38. Jones, *Corregidora*, 129.

39. Ibid., 79.

40. Ibid., 78.

41. Ibid., 22.
42. Ibid., 14.
43. Felman and Laub, *Testimony*, 57.
44. Harris, "Gayl Jones: *Corregidora*," 44.
45. Ibid., 40.
46. Ibid., 56.
47. Ibid., 54.
48. Ibid., 77.
49. Ibid., 59.
50. Ibid., 67.
51. Ibid., 102.
52. Ibid.
53. Ibid., 103.
54. Ibid., 104.
55. Ibid., 120.
56. Ibid., 132.
57. Simon, "Traumatic Repetition," 102–3.
58. Dubey, "Gayl Jones," 252.
59. Hirsch, "Surviving Images," 8–9.
60. Abraham, "Notes on the Phantom," 287.
61. Herman, *Trauma and Recovery*, 211.

5 / "I Have Never Seen a Movie Like That"

1. In "Landscapes of Memory: Trauma, Narrative, and Dissociation," Laurence Kirmayer describes the popular comparison between memory and photography: "In one common version, memories are 'snapshots,' laid down at the time of experience through a process of registration. They persist unchanged throughout our lives to be recalled when we look for them, like opening a photo album" (176).

2. Nora, "Between Memory and History," 8.

3. Noteworthy scholarly explorations of the relationship between individual and cultural response to traumatic experience include the following texts: Miller and Tougaw, *Extremities*; Caruth, *Trauma*; Antze and Lambek, *Tense Past*; van der Kolk, McFarlane, and Weisaeth, *Traumatic Stress*; Herman, *Trauma and Recovery*; and Felman, *The Juridical Unconscious*.

4. This chapter uses the Anchor Books/Doubleday text and the PBS video production of *Twilight* because these resources are the most widely available for students, teachers, and scholars interested in Smith's work.

5. Nora, "Between Memory and History," 17.

6. Friedman, "Making History," 12–13.

7. For an analysis of the role of media in Smith's work, see Callen's "Staging the Televised (Nation)."

8. Nora, "Between Memory and History," 8.

9. Laurino, "Sensitivity Comes 'from the Soles of the Feet,'" 43. Peggy Phelan suggests that "in a certain sense, Smith's performance seeks to preserve and contain the chaotic flood of images the cameras 'mechanically' reproduced. . . . Camera images may need to re-enter the space of theatre in order to be arrested, arranged, digested, comprehended, 'explained'" ("Arresting Performances of Sexual and Racial

Difference," 6–7). In Phelan's argument, the camera images provide the raw material of crisis a framework in which it can be read and understood. With the "flood of chaotic images," the camera signifies the level of traumatic memory that also appears to be "mechanically reproduced," immutable, relentless flashbacks within the consciousness of the survivor.

10. Smith, *Twilight: Los Angeles, 1992*, 66.

11. Ibid., 62.

12. Ibid., 65.

13. Ibid.

14. In "Rodney King, Shifting Modes of Vision and Anna Deavere Smith's *Twilight: Los Angeles, 1992*," Robin Bernstein describes *Twilight* as resisting a "cybernetic mode of vision" that renders the referent of the visual image and the subjectivity of the observer irrelevant. This mode of vision was enacted, according to Bernstein, in the courtroom by the police officers' defense attorneys, the "authorities [who] must provide the referent," when they interpreted the beating through the process of reading frame by frame.

15. Tomasulo, "I'll See It When I Believe It," 78.

16. Hirsch defines and examines the term *postmemory* specifically in relation to second-generation Holocaust survivors.

17. Hirsch, "Surviving Images," 8–9.

18. For a compelling analysis of Hirsch's concept of postmemory in relation to collective trauma, testimony, and theater, see Francine A'ness's "Resisting Amnesia."

19. Baker, "Scene . . . Not Heard," 40.

20. Phelan, "Arresting Performances of Sexual and Racial Difference," 6–7.

21. Fanon, *Black Skin, White Masks*, 116.

22. Ibid., 111. The discussion of the "historico-racial schema" occurs in a well-known passage of *Black Skin, White Masks*, cited previously in the introduction and in chapter 3, in which Fanon encounters a young white child in a public setting, and the child expresses fear, points at Fanon, and exclaims, "Look, a Negro!"

23. Smith, *Fires in the Mirror*, xxv.

24. Nora, "Between Memory and History," 13.

25. Felman and Laub, *Testimony*, 24.

26. Schechner, "Anna Deavere Smith," 64.

27. Nora, "Between Memory and History," 17.

28. Smith, *Twilight*, xx.

29. Laub, "Truth and Testimony," 61.

30. Ibid.

31. Felman and Laub, *Testimony*, 17.

32. In *Talk to Me*, Smith describes her desire to move away the Stanislavsky technique, which she refers to as "a spiritual dead end" (53) because it erases difference. "I wanted to find other ways of getting inside of a person. I don't think I should base my idea of another person all on my own feelings" (53).

33. Malpede, "Teaching Witnessing," 168–69.

34. van der Kolk, "Trauma and Memory," 280.

35. Felman and Laub, *Testimony*, 5.

36. Bourne, "Actress/Writer Seeks Poetry in Everyday People's Expression," 15.

37. Quoted in Laurino, "Sensitivity," 43.

38. From PBS recording of a performance of *Twilight,* transcribed by the author.

39. Felman and Laub, *Testimony,* 5.

40. Gilman, "Truth Seeking, Memory, and Art."

41. Salverson, "Performing Emergency," 188.

42. Martin, "Anna Deavere Smith," 190.

43. Richards, "Caught in the Act of Social Definition," 35.

44. Kondo, "(Re)Visions of Race," 98.

45. Layton, "Trauma, Gender Identity, and Sexuality," 117.

46. Ibid., 114.

47. Bhabha, *The Location of Culture,* 12.

48. Erickson, "Notes on Trauma and Community," 186.

49. Ainslie and Brabeck, "Race Murder and Community Trauma," 47.

50. Mitchell, "Trauma, Recognition, and the Place of Language," 121.

51. Ibid., 121. Mitchell describes the experience as one void of content on a symbolic level: "Trauma makes a breach that empties the person out; probably after the gasp of emptiness, there is rage or hatred—an identification with the violence of the shock. This state cannot be lived with; quite often it is evacuated, and then a phony or pseudo state will be resorted to" (ibid., 159). The failure of the symbolic order to accommodate traumatic experience results in the "phony or pseudo state," which I suggest corresponds with the media representation of the trial's violent aftermath.

52. Smith, *Twilight,* 190.

53. Mitchell, "Trauma, Recognition, and the Place of Language," 151.

54. Herman, *Trauma and Recovery,* 133.

55. "Early on in my work," Smith explains, "I wanted to use my body as evidence that a human being can take on the identity of another. . . . I think we have immense potential for compassion as individuals. But that gets stopped when we take on fixed positions." Berson, "Ethnic Bonds Can Be Limiting," A13.

56. Smith, *Twilight,* 16.

57. Ibid., 3.

58. Ibid., 6.

59. Ibid., 125–27.

60. Ibid., 35.

61. Ibid., 39.

62. Ibid., 52.

63. Chun, "Unbearable Witness," 17.

64. Phelan, *Unmarked,* 13.

65. Wu, *Yellow,* 28.

66. Kondo, "(Re)visions of Race," 97.

67. Perea, "The Black/White Binary Paradigm of Race," 346.

68. Smith, *Twilight,* xxiii. See also Kondo, "Shades of Twilight."

69. Ikemoto, "Traces of the Master Narrative in the Story of African American/Korean American Conflict," 302.

70. Smith, *Twilight,* 142.

71. Ibid., 147.

72. Ibid., 245.

73. Wu, *Yellow,* 72.

74. Lowe, *Immigrant Acts,* 91.

75. Ibid., 96.

76. Nora, "Between Memory and History," 7. After identifying in Nora "a Euro-centric bias in favor of recorded historical analysis when he considers non-Europe-ans," Melvin Dixon engages Nora's *lieux de memoire* to examine the complex relation-ship between history and sites of memory in African American cultural productions. Dixon, "The Black Writer's Use of Memory," 18.

77. Smith, *Twilight*, 111.

78. Ibid., 177.

79. Ibid.

80. Matsuda, *Where Is Your Body?* 90.

81. Ibid., 96.

82. Liu, "The Female Body and Nationalist Discourse," 37.

83. Robben, "How Traumatized Societies Remember," 127.

84. Quoted in Laurino, "Sensitivity Comes 'from the Soles of the Feet,'" 43.

85. McFarlane and van der Kolk, "Trauma and Its Challenge to Society," 41.

86. Abraham and Torok, *The Shell and the Kernel*, 189.

Bibliography

Abraham, Nicholas. "Notes on the Phantom: A Complement to Freud's Metapsychology." Translated by Nicholas Rand. *Critical Inquiry* 13, no. 2 (1987): 287–92.

Abraham, Nicholas, and Maria Torok. *The Shell and the Kernel.* Vol. 1. Ed. and trans. Nicholas T. Rand. Chicago: U of Chicago P, 1994.

Ainslie, Ricardo, and Kalina Brabeck. "Race Murder and Community Trauma: Psychoanalysis and Ethnography in Exploring the Impact of the Killing of James Byrd in Jasper, Texas." *Journal for the Psychoanalysis of Culture and Society* 8, no. 1 (2003): 42–50.

Altrick, Richard. *The Shows of London.* Cambridge, MA: Harvard UP, 1978.

A'ness, Francine. "Resisting Amnesia: Yuyachkani, Performance, and the Postwar Reconstruction of Peru." *Theatre Journal* 56 (2004): 395–414.

Antze, Paul, and Michael Lambek, eds. *Tense Past: Cultural Essays in Trauma and Memory.* New York: Routledge, 1996.

Anzaldúa, Gloria. *Borderlands/La Frontera: The New Mestiza.* Boston: Aunt Lute Books, 1987.

Bakare-Yusuf, Bibi. "The Economy of Violence: Black Bodies and the Unspeakable Terror." In *Gender and Catastrophe*, edited by Ronit Lentin, 311–23. London: Zed Books, 1997. Rpt. in *Feminist Theory and the Body*, edited by Janet Price and Margrit Shildrick. New York: Routledge, 1999.

Baker, Houston. "Scene . . . Not Heard." In *Reading Rodney King: Reading Urban Uprising*, edited by Robert Gooding-Williams, 38–50. New York: Routledge, 1997.

Bartky, Sandra Lee. "The Pedagogy of Shame." In *Feminisms and Pedagogies of Everyday Life*, edited by Carmen Luke, 225–41. Albany: State U of New York P, 1996.

Berenstein, Robin. "Rodney King, Shifting Modes of Vision and Anna Deavere Smith's *Twilight: Los Angeles, 1992.*" *Journal of Dramatic Theory and Criticism* 14, no. 2 (2000): 121–34.

Berson, Misha. "Ethnic Bonds Can Be Limiting, Actress Tells Race Forum." *Seattle Times,* 21 Nov. 1998, A13.

Bhabha, Homi. *The Location of Culture.* London: Routledge, 1994.

Bourne, Kay. "Actress/Writer Seeks Poetry in Everyday People's Expression." *Ethnic Newswatch, Bay State Banner* 32, no. 31 (1 May 1997).

Bronfen, Elisabeth. "From Omphalos to Phallus: Cultural Representations of Femininity and Death." *Women: A Cultural Review* 3, no. 2 (1992): 145–58.

Bronfen, Elisabeth. *Over Her Dead Body: Death, Femininity and the Aesthetic.* New York: Routledge, 1992.

Brooks Bouson, J. *Quiet as It's Kept: Shame, Trauma, and Race in the Novels of Toni Morrison.* Albany: State U of New York P, 1999.

Brown, Laura S. "Not Outside the Range: One Feminist Perspective on Psychic Trauma." In *Trauma: Explorations in Memory,* edited by Cathy Caruth, 100–112. Baltimore: Johns Hopkins UP, 1995.

Brownmiller, Susan. *Against Our Will: Men, Women, and Rape.* New York: Simon and Schuster, 1975.

Butler, Judith. "Endangered/Endangering: Schematic Racism and White Paranoia." In *Reading Rodney King: Reading Urban Uprising,* edited by Robert Gooding-Williams, 15–22. New York: Routledge, 1997.

Callen, Johan. "Staging the Televised (Nation)." *Theatre Research International* 28 (2003): 61–78.

Caruth, Cathy. "An Interview with Robert Jay Lifton." In *Trauma: Explorations in Memory,* edited by Cathy Caruth, 128–50. Baltimore: Johns Hopkins UP, 1995.

Caruth, Cathy. *Trauma: Explorations in Memory.* Baltimore: Johns Hopkins UP, 1995.

Caruth, Cathy. *Unclaimed Experience: Trauma, Narrative, History.* Baltimore: Johns Hopkins UP, 1996.

Caruth, Cathy, and Thomas Keenan. "'The AIDS Crisis Is Not Over': A Conversation with Gregg Bordowitz, Douglas Crimp, and Laura Pinsky." In *Trauma: Explorations in Memory,* edited by Cathy Caruth, 256–72. Baltimore: Johns Hopkins UP, 1995.

Christensen, Kimberly. "'With Whom Do You Believe Your Lot Is Cast?': White Feminists and Racism." *Signs* 22, no. 3 (1997): 617–48.

Chun, Wendy Hui. "Unbearable Witness: Toward a Politics of Listening." *Differences: A Journal of Feminist Cultural Studies* 11, no. 1 (1999): 112–49.

Culbertson, Roberta. "Embodied Memory, Transcendence, and Telling: Recounting Trauma, Reestablishing the Self." *New Literary History* 26 (1995): 169–95.

Davis, Angela. *Woman, Race, and Class*. New York: Vintage, 1981.

de Certeau, Michel. *The Practices of Everyday Life*. Trans. Steven Rendell. Berkeley: U of California P, 1984.

Demleitner, N. V. "The Law at a Crossroads: The Construction of Migrant Women Trafficked into Prostitution." In *Global Human Smuggling: Comparative Perspectives*, edited by D. Kyle and R. Koslowski, 257–93. Baltimore: Johns Hopkins UP, 2001.

Diamond, Elin. *Unmaking Mimesis: Essays on Feminism and Theater*. New York: Routledge, 1997.

Dixon, Melvin. "The Black Writer's Use of Memory." In *History and Memory in African-American Culture*, edited by Geneviève Fabre and Robert O'Meally, 18–27. New York: Oxford UP, 1994.

Dolan, Jill. *The Feminist Spectator as Critic*. Ann Arbor: U of Michigan P, 1991.

Douglass, Ana, and Thomas A. Vogler. *Witness and Memory: The Discourse of Trauma*. New York: Routledge, 2003.

Dubey, Madhu. "Gayl Jones and the Matrilineal Metaphor of Tradition." *Signs* 20, no. 2 (1995): 296–307.

Elam, Harry, and Alice Rayner. "Body Parts: Between Story and Spectacle in *Venus* by Suzan-Lori Parks." In *Staging Resistance*, edited by Jeanne Colleran and Jenny Spencer, 265–82. Ann Arbor: U of Michigan P, 1998.

Erickson, Kai. "Notes on Trauma and Community." In *Trauma: Explorations in Memory*, edited by Cathy Caruth, 183–99. Baltimore: Johns Hopkins UP, 1995.

Eyerman, Ron. *Cultural Trauma: Slavery and the Formation of African American Identity*. New York: Cambridge UP, 2001.

Fanon, Frantz. *Black Skin, White Masks*. Trans. Charles Lam Markmann. New York: Grove, 1967.

Fausto-Sterling, Anne. "Gender, Race, and Nation: The Comparative Anatomy of 'Hottentot' Women in Europe, 1815–1817." In *Deviant Bodies: Critical Perspectives on Difference in Science and Popular Culture*, edited by Jennifer Terry and Jacqueline Urla, 19–48. Bloomington: Indiana UP, 1995.

Felman, Shoshana. *The Juridical Unconscious: Trials and Traumas in the Twentieth Century*. Cambridge, MA: Harvard UP, 2002.

Felman, Shoshana, and Dori Laub. *Testimony: Crises of Witnessing in Literature, Psychoanalysis, and History*. New York: Routledge, 1994.

Forte, Jeanie. "Focus on the Body: Pain, Praxis, and Pleasure in Feminist Performance." In *Critical Theory and Performance*, edited by Jannelle G. Reinelt and Joseph R. Roach, 248–62. Ann Arbor: U of Michigan P, 1992.

Foucault, Michel. *Language, Counter-Memory, Practice*. Ed. Donald F. Bouchard. Trans. Donald F. Bouchard and Sherry Simon. Ithaca, NY: Cornell UP, 1977.

Frankenberg, Ruth. "'When We Are Capable of Stopping, We Begin to See': Being White, Seeing Whiteness." In *Names We Call Home: Autobiography on*

Racial Identity, edited by Becky Thompson and Sangeeta Tyagi, 3–18. New York: Routledge, 1996.

Frankenberg, Ruth. *White Women, Race Matters: The Social Construction of Whiteness.* Minneapolis: U of Minnesota P, 1993.

Freud, Sigmund. "The Uncanny." In *The Standard Edition of the Complete Psychological Works of Sigmund Freud.* Vol. 17. Trans. and ed. James Strachey, 219–52. London: Hogarth, 1953.

Freyd, Jennifer. *Betrayal Trauma.* Cambridge, MA: Harvard UP, 1996.

Friedman, Susan Stanford. "Making History: Reflections on Feminism, Narrative, and Desire." In *Feminism Beside Itself,* edited by Diane Elam and Robyn Wiegman, 11–54. New York: Routledge, 1995.

Friedman, Susan Stanford. "Beyond White and Other: Relationality and Narratives of Race in Feminist Discourse." *Signs* 21, no. 1 (1995): 1–49.

Gilbert, Sandra, and Susan Gubar. *The Madwoman in the Attic: The Woman Writer and the Nineteenth-Century Literary Imagination.* New Haven, CT: Yale UP, 1980.

Gilman, Sander. "Truth Seeking, Memory, and Art: Comments Following Four Weeks of Life in the New South Africa." In *Africus Johannesburg Biennale Catalogue,* edited by Allan Boyer and Candace Breitz, 36–38. Johannesburg: Transitional Metropolitan Council, 1995.

Goldberg, Elizabeth Swanson. "Living the Legacy: Pain, Desire, and Narrative Time in Gayl Jones' *Corregidora.*" *Callaloo: A Journal of African-American and African Arts and Letters* 26, no. 2 (2003): 446–72.

Griffin, Farah Jasmine. "Textual Healing: Claiming Black Women's Bodies, the Erotic, and Resistance in Contemporary Novels of Slavery." *Callaloo: A Journal of African-American and African Arts and Letters* 19, no. 2 (1999): 519–36.

Gutierrez-Jones, Carl, *Critical Race Narratives.* New York: New York UP, 2001.

Hammonds, Evelynn M. "Toward a Genealogy of Black Female Sexuality: The Problematic of Silence." In *Feminist Genealogies, Colonial Legacies, Democratic Futures,* edited by M. Jacqui Alexander and Chandra Talpade Mohanty, 170–82. New York: Routledge, 1997.

Harris, Hilary. "Failing 'White Woman': Interrogating the Performance of Respectability." *Theatre Journal* 52, no. 2 (2000): 183–209.

Harris, Janice. "Gayl Jones: *Corregidora.*" *Frontiers: A Journal of Women's Studies* 5, no. 3 (1980): 1–5.

Hayward, Ian, and Zachary Leader. *Romantic Period Writings, 1798–1832.* New York: Routledge, 1998.

Henderson, Mae. "Speaking in Tongues: Dialogics, Dialectics, and the Black Women Writers' Literary Tradition." In *Changing Our Words: Essays on Criticism, Theory, and Writing by Black Women,* edited by Cheryl Wall, 16–37. New Brunswick, NJ: Rutgers UP, 1989.

Herman, Judith. *Trauma and Recovery: The Aftermath of Violence—from Domestic Violence to Political Terror.* New York: Basic Books, 1992.

Hirsch, Marianne. "Surviving Images: Holocaust Photographs and the Works of Postmemory." *Yale Journal of Criticism* 14, no. 1 (2001): 5–37.

hooks, bell. "Feminism as a Persistent Critique of History: What's Love Got to Do with It?" In *The Fact of Blackness: Frantz Fanon and Visual Representation*, edited by Alan Read, 338–46. Seattle: Bay Press, 1996.

hooks, bell. "Representing Whiteness in the Black Imagination." In *Cultural Studies*, edited by Lawrence Grossberg, Cary Nelson, and Paula Treichler, 76–85. New York: Routledge, 1992.

Ikemoto, Lisa C. "Traces of the Master Narrative in the Story of African American/Korean American Conflict: How We Constructed 'Los Angeles.'" In *Critical Race Theory*, 2nd ed., edited by Richard Delgado and Jean Stefancic, 302–12. Philadelphia: Temple UP, 2000.

Jones, Gayl. *Corregidora.* Boston: Beacon, 1975.

King, Deborah Walker. *African Americans and the Culture of Pain.* Charlottesville: U of Virginia P, 2008.

Kirmayer, Laurence J. "Landscapes of Memory: Trauma, Narrative, and Dissociation." In *Tense Past: Cultural Essays in Trauma and Memory*, edited by Paul Antze and Michael Lambek, 173–98. New York: Routledge, 1996.

Kondo, Dorinne. "(Re)Visions of Race: Contemporary Race Theory and the Cultural Politics of Racial Crossover in Documentary Theatre." *Theatre Journal* 52, no. 1 (2000): 81–107.

Kondo, Dorinne. "Shades of Twilight: Anna Deavere Smith and *Twilight: Los Angeles, 1992*." In *Late Editions 3: Connected: Engagements with Media*, edited by George Marcus, 313–46. Chicago: U of Chicago P, 1996.

LaCapra, Dominick. *Writing History, Writing Trauma.* Baltimore: Johns Hopkins UP, 2001.

Laub, Dori. "Truth and Testimony: The Process and the Struggle." In *Trauma: Explorations in Memory*, edited by Cathy Caruth, 61–75. Baltimore: Johns Hopkins UP, 1995

Laurino, Maria. "Sensitivity Comes 'from the Soles of the Feet.'" *Newsday*, 23 Feb. 1994, 43.

Layton, Lynne. "Trauma, Gender Identity, and Sexuality: Discourses on Fragmentation." *American Imago* 2, no. 1 (1995): 107–25.

Lerner, Gerda, ed. *Black Women in White America: A Documentary History.* New York: Vintage, 1972.

Lifton, Robert Jay. *Nazi Doctors: Medical Killing and the Psychology of Genocide.* New York: Perseus, 1986.

Liu, Lydia. "The Female Body and Nationalist Discourse: *The Field of Life and Death* Revisited." In *Scattered Hegemonies: Postmodern and Transnational Feminist Practices*, edited by Inderpal Grewal and Caren Kaplan, 157–80. Minneapolis: U of Minnesota P, 1994.

"Look beneath the Surface." U.S. Department of Health and Human Services, Administration of Children and Families, http://www.acf.hhs.gov/trafficking/campaign_kits/tool_kit_health/health_care_brochure.pdf.

Louis, Yvette. "Body Language: The Black Female Body and the Word in Suzan-Lori Parks's *The Last Black Man in the Whole Entire World.*" In *Recovering the Black Female Body: Self-Representations by African American Women,* edited by Michael Bennett and Vanessa D. Dickerson, 141–64. New Brunswick, NJ: Rutgers UP, 2001.

Lowe, Lisa. *Immigrant Acts.* Durham, NC: Duke UP, 1996.

Malpede, Karen. "Teaching Witnessing: A Class Wakes to Genocide." *Theatre Topics* 6, no. 2 (1996): 167–79.

Marneweck, Aja. "Staging Stereotype and Performing the Exotic Erotic: An Interrogation of Desire in the Texts of Parks and Kennedy." *South African Theatre Journal* 18 (2004): 50–64.

Martin, Carol. "Anna Deavere Smith: The Word Becomes You." In *A Sourcebook for Feminist Theatre and Performance: On and Beyond the Stage,* edited by Carol Martin, 81–93. New York: Routledge, 1996.

Masson, J. M. *The Assault on Truth: Freud's Suppression of the Seduction Theory.* New York: Farrar, Straus, and Giroux, 1984.

Matsuda, Mari. *Where Is Your Body? and Other Essays on Race, Gender, and the Law.* Boston: Beacon, 1996.

McCauley, Robbie. *Sally's Rape.* Performance on PBS's *Conjure Women,* directed by Demetria Royals and produced by Louise Diamond. PBS video, 1995.

McCauley, Robbie. *Sally's Rape.* In *Moon Marked and Touched by the Sun,* edited by Sydne Mahone, 211–38. New York: Theatre Communications Group, 1994.

McCauley, Robbie. "Thoughts on My Career, *The Other Weapon,* and Other Projects." In *Performance and Cultural Politics,* edited by Elin Diamond, 267–84. London: Routledge, 1996.

McFarlane, Alexander C., and Bessel A. van der Kolk. "Trauma and Its Challenge to Society." In *Traumatic Stress: The Effects of Overwhelming Experience on Mind, Body, and Society,* edited by Bessel A. van der Kolk, Alexander C. McFarlane, and Lars Weisaeth, 24–46. New York: Guilford, 1996.

McKay, Nellie. "Alice Walker's 'Advancing Luna—and Ida B. Wells': A Struggle toward Sisterhood." In *Rape and Representation,* edited by Lynn A. Higgins and Brenda R. Silver, 248–62. New York: Columbia UP, 1991.

Mercer, Kobena. "Dialogue." In *The Fact of Blackness: Frantz Fanon and Visual Representation,* edited by Alan Read, 114–31. Seattle: Bay Press, 1996.

Miller, Gregory. "The Bottom of Desire in Suzan-Lori Parks's *Venus.*" *Modern Drama* 45, no. 1 (Spring 2002): 125–37.

Miller, Nancy, and Jason Tougaw, eds. *Extremities: Trauma, Testimony, and Community.* Urbana: U of Illinois P, 2002.

Mitchell, Juliet. "Trauma, Recognition, and the Place of Language." *Diacritics* 28, no. 4 (1998): 121–33.

Morgenstern, Naomi. "Mother's Milk and Sister's Blood: Trauma and the Neo-slave Narrative." *Differences: A Journal of Feminist Cultural Studies* 8, no. 2 (1996): 101–26.

Morrison, Toni. *Playing the Dark: Whiteness and the Literary Imagination.* New York: Vintage, 1992.

Nadar, Kathleen Olympia. "Violence: Effects of Parents' Previous Trauma on Currently Traumatized Children." In *International Handbook of Multigenerational Legacies of Trauma,* edited by Yael Danieli, 571–86. New York: Plenum, 1998.

Nora, Pierre. "Between Memory and History: Les Lieux de Memoire." Trans. Marc Roudebush. *Representations* 26 (Spring 1989): 7–24.

Nymann, Ann E. "*Sally's Rape*: Robbie McCauley's Survival Art," *African American Review* 33, no. 4 (1999): 577–87.

Parks, Suzan-Lori. *Venus.* New York: Theatre Communications Group, 1997.

Patraka, Vivian. "Robbie McCauley: Obsessing in Public: An Interview with Vivian Patraka." *TDR (The Drama Review)* 37, no. 2 (1993): 25–55. Rpt. in *A Sourcebook of Feminist Theatre and Performance: On and Beyond the Stage,* edited by Carol Martin, 205–38. New York: Routledge, 1996.

Perea, Juan F. "The Black/White Binary Paradigm of Race." In *Critical Race Theory,* 2nd ed., edited by Richard Delgado and Jean Stefancic, 344–53. Philadelphia: Temple UP, 2000.

Phelan, Peggy. "Arresting Performances of Sexual and Racial Difference: Toward a Theory of Performative Film." *Women and Performance* 6, no. 2 (1993): 5–10.

Phelan, Peggy. *Unmarked: The Politics of Performance.* London: Routledge, 1993.

Pierce-Baker, Charlotte. *Surviving Silence: Black Women's Stories of Rape.* New York: Norton, 1998.

Richards, Sandra L. "Caught in the Act of Social Definition: On the Road with Anna Deavere Smith." In *Acting Out: Feminist Performances,* edited by Lynda Hart and Peggy Phelan, 35–54. Ann Arbor: U of Michigan P, 1993.

Roach, Joseph. *Cities of the Dead: Circum-Atlantic Performance.* New York: Columbia UP, 1996.

Robben, Antonius C. G. M. "How Traumatized Societies Remember: The Aftermath of Argentina's Dirty War." *Cultural Critique* 59 (2005): 120–64.

Root, Maria. "Reconstructing the Impact of Trauma on Personality." In *Personality and Psychopathology: Feminist Reappraisals,* edited by Laura S. Brown and Mary Ballou, 229–65. New York: Guilford, 1992.

Rosenfeld, Megan. "Spectators at Stage Center: McCauley Makes Audience Part of Her Performances." *Washington Post,* 5 May 1994, D2.

Rubin, Gayl S. "Thinking Sex: Notes for a Radical Theory of the Politics of

Sexuality." In *The Lesbian and Gay Studies Reader,* edited by Henry Abelove, Michèle Aina Barale, and David M. Halperin, 3–44. New York: Routledge, 1993.

Rushdy, Ashraf H. A. *Neoslave Narratives: Studies in the Social Logic of Literary Form.* New York: Oxford UP, 1999.

Sanchez, Marta. "The Estrangement Effect in Sherley Anne Williams' Dessa Rose." *Genders* 15 (1992): 21–36.

Salverson, Julie. "Performing Emergency: Witnessing, Popular Theatre, and the Lie of the Literal." *Theatre Topics* 6, no. 2 (1996): 181–91.

Scarry, Elaine. *The Body in Pain: The Making and Unmaking of the World.* Oxford: Oxford UP, 1987.

Schaffer, Kay, and Sidonie Smith. "Conjunctions: Life Narratives in the Field of Human Rights." *Biography: An Interdisciplinary Quarterly* 27, no. 1 (2004): 1–24.

Schechner, Richard. "Anna Deavere Smith: Acting as Incorporation." *TDR (The Drama Review)* 37, no. 4 (1993): 63–64.

Schiebinger, Londa. *Nature's Body: Gender and the Making of Modern Science.* New Brunswick, NJ: Rutgers UP, 2004.

Schneider, Rebecca. *The Explicit Body in Performance.* New York: Routledge, 1997.

Sharpley-Whiting, T. Denean. *Black Venus: Sexualized Savages, Primal Fears, and Primitive Narratives in French.* Durham, NC: Duke UP, 1999.

Simon, Bruce. "Traumatic Repetition: Gayl Jones's *Corregidora.*" In *Race Consciousness: African-American Studies for the New Century,* edited by Judith Jackson Fossett and Jeffrey A. Tucker, 93–112. New York: New York UP, 1997.

Smith, Anna Deavere. *Fires in the Mirror: Crown Heights, Brooklyn, and Other Identities.* New York: Anchor Books, 1993.

Smith, Anna Deavere. *Talk to Me: Listening between the Lines.* New York: Random House, 2000.

Smith, Anna Deavere. *Twilight: Los Angeles, 1992.* New York: Anchor Books, 1994.

Smith, Joan. "Why British Men Are Rapists." *New Statesman,* 23 Jan. 2006, 15.

Smith, Valerie. "Split Affinities: The Case of Interracial Rape." In *Conflicts in Feminism,* edited by Marianne Hirsch and Evelyn Fox Keller, 271–87. New York: Routledge, 1990.

Spillers, Hortense. "'All the Things You Could Be by Now, If Sigmund Freud's Wife Was Your Mother': Psychoanalysis and Race." In *Female Subjects in Black and White: Race, Psychoanalysis, Feminism,* edited by Elizabeth Abel, Barbara Christian, and Helene Moglen, 135–58. Berkeley: U of California P, 1997.

Tate, Claudia. *Psychoanalysis and Black Novels: Desire and the Protocols of Race.* Oxford: Oxford UP, 1998.

Taussig, Michael. *The Nervous System*. New York: Routledge, 1992 .

Thompson, Deborah. "Blackface, Rape, and Beyond: Rehearsing Interracial Dialogue in *Sally's Rape*." *Theatre Journal* 48, no. 2 (1996): 123–39.

Todd, Janet. "The Veiled Woman in Freud's Das Unheimliche." *Signs* 11, no. 3 (1986): 519–28.

Tomasulo, Frank. "'I'll See It When I Believe It': Rodney King and the Prison-House of Video." In *The Persistence of History: Cinema, Television, and the Modern Event*, edited by Vivian Sobchack, 69–90. New York: Routledge, 1996.

Trinh T. Minh-ha. *Woman, Native, Other: Writing Postcoloniality and Feminism*. Bloomington: Indiana UP, 1989.

van der Kolk, Bessel A. "Trauma and Memory." In *Traumatic Stress: The Effects of Overwhelming Experience on Mind, Body, and Society*, edited by Bessel A. van der Kolk, Alexander C. McFarlane, and Lars Weisaeth, 279–302. New York: Guilford, 1996.

van der Kolk, Bessel A., Alexander C. McFarlane, and Lars Weisaeth, eds. *Traumatic Stress: The Effects of Overwhelming Experience on the Mind, Body, and Society*. New York: Guilford, 1996.

Warner, Sara L. "Suzan-Lori Parks's Drama of Disinternment: A Transnational Exploration of Venus." *Theatre Journal* 60, no. 2 (2008): 181–99.

Williams, Sherley Anne. *Give Birth to Brightness: A Thematic Study of Neo-Black Literature*. New York: Dial, 1972.

Williams, Sherley Anne. *Dessa Rose*. New York: Berkeley Books, 1986.

Wu, Frank. *Yellow: Race in America beyond Black and White*. New York: Basic Books, 2002.

Young, Harvey. "Touching History: Suzan-Lori Parks, Robbie McCauley, and the Black Body." *Text and Performance Quarterly* 23, no. 2 (2003): 133–52.

Young, Jean. "The Re-objectification and Re-commodification of Saartjie Baartman in Suzan-Lori Parks's *Venus*," *African American Review* 31, no. 4 (1997): 699–708.

Yukins, Elizabeth. "Bastard Daughters and the Possession of History in *Corregidora* and *Paradise*." *Signs* 28, no. 1 (2002): 221–47.

Zook, Kristal Brent. *Black Women's Lives: Stories of Power and Pain*. New York: Nation Books, 2006.

Zwarg, Christine. "Du Bois on Trauma: Psychoanalysis and the Would-Be Black Savant." *Cultural Critique* 51 (2002): 1–39.

Index